Prepare your favorite colors, sharp your colored pencils and dive into the fun of coloring! Each page of this book features a unique butterfly, ready to come to life with your creativity. Explore different color combinations and create your own works of art while learning about these incredible creatures of nature.

This book, made by AI, is dedicated to all nature lovers, big and small, who find beauty and inspiration in the small wonders around us. May your coloring journey be full of joy, creativity and discoveries about the magical world of butterflies.

Color Test

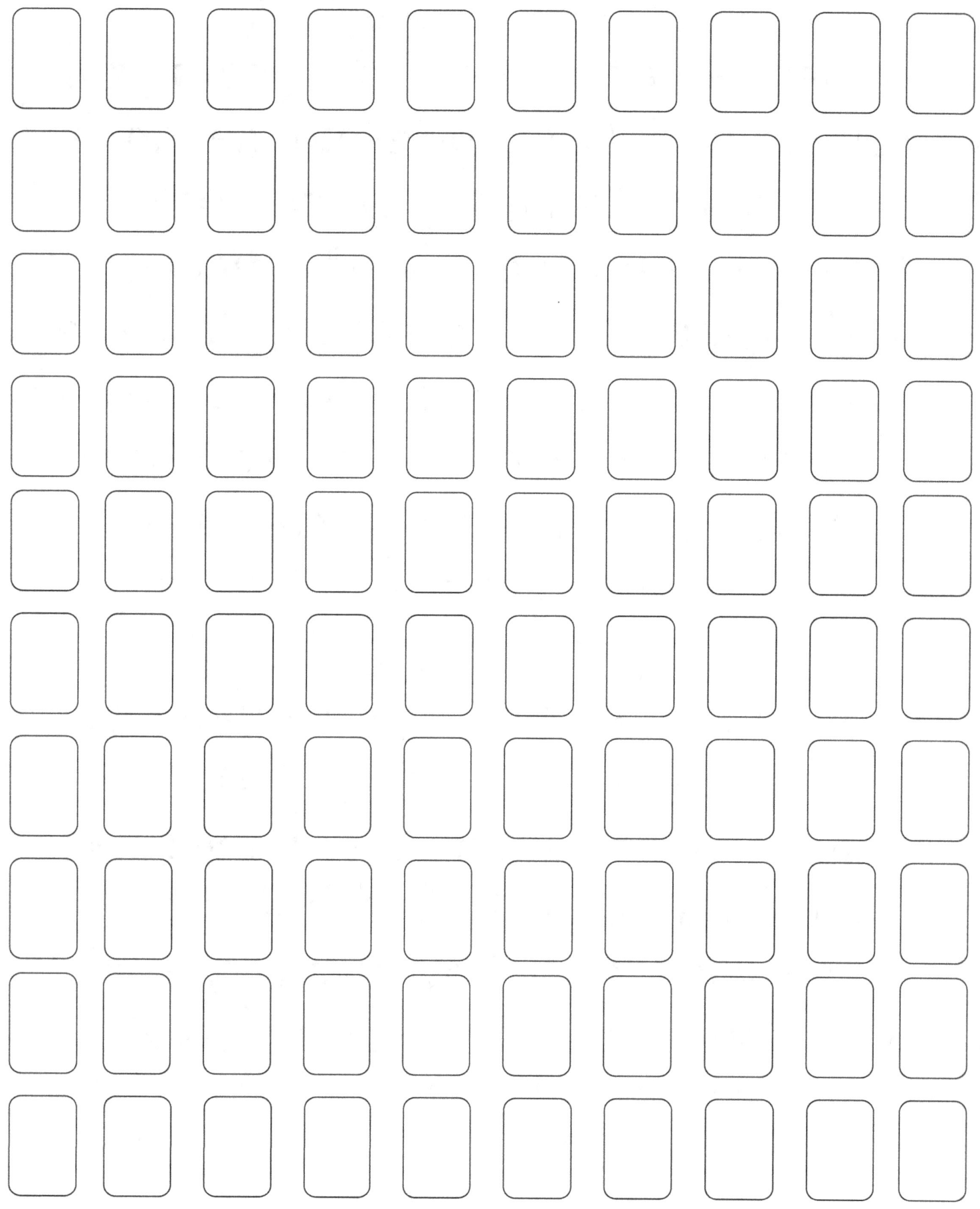

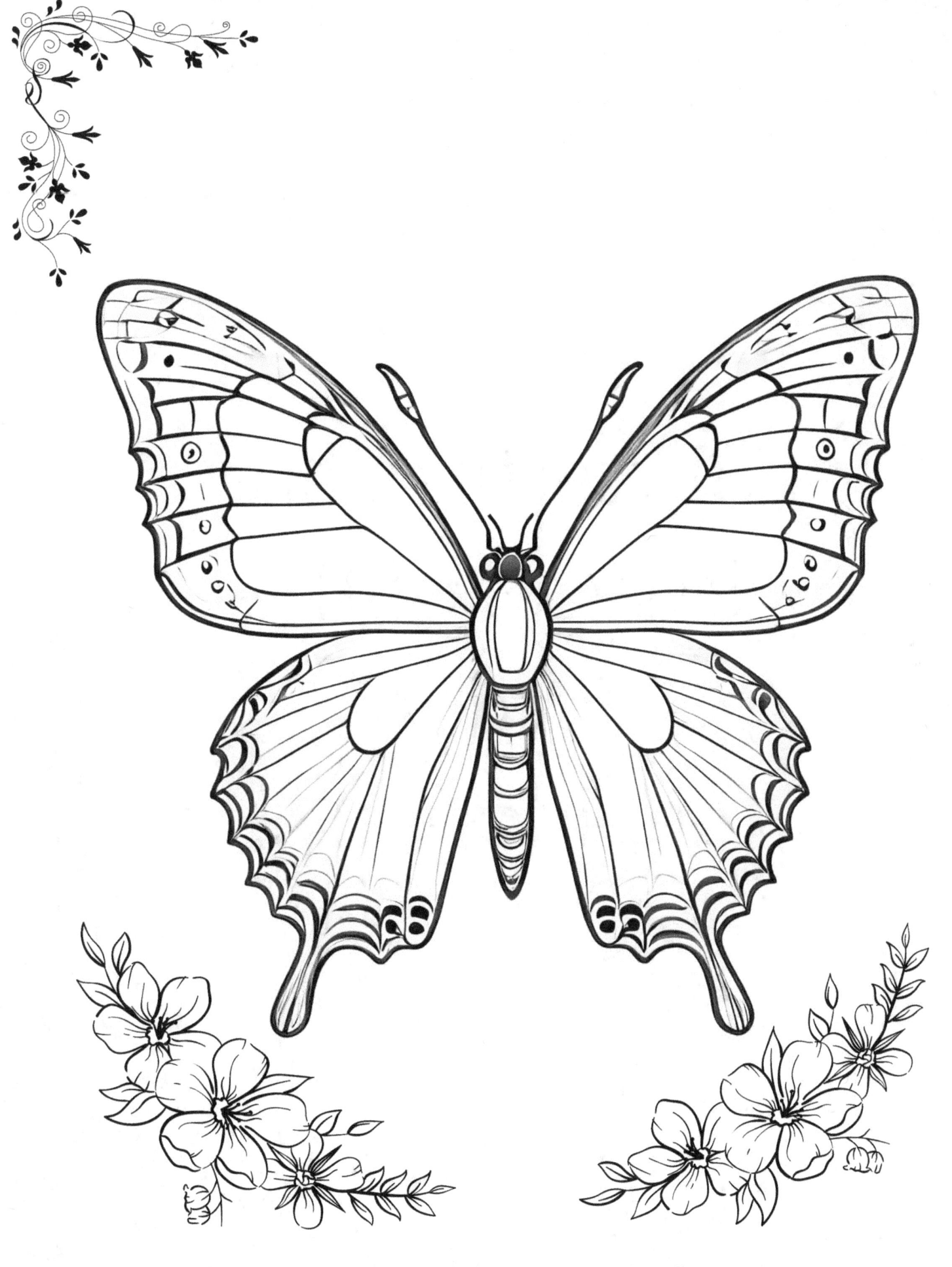

Butterflies are insects of the order Lepidoptera.

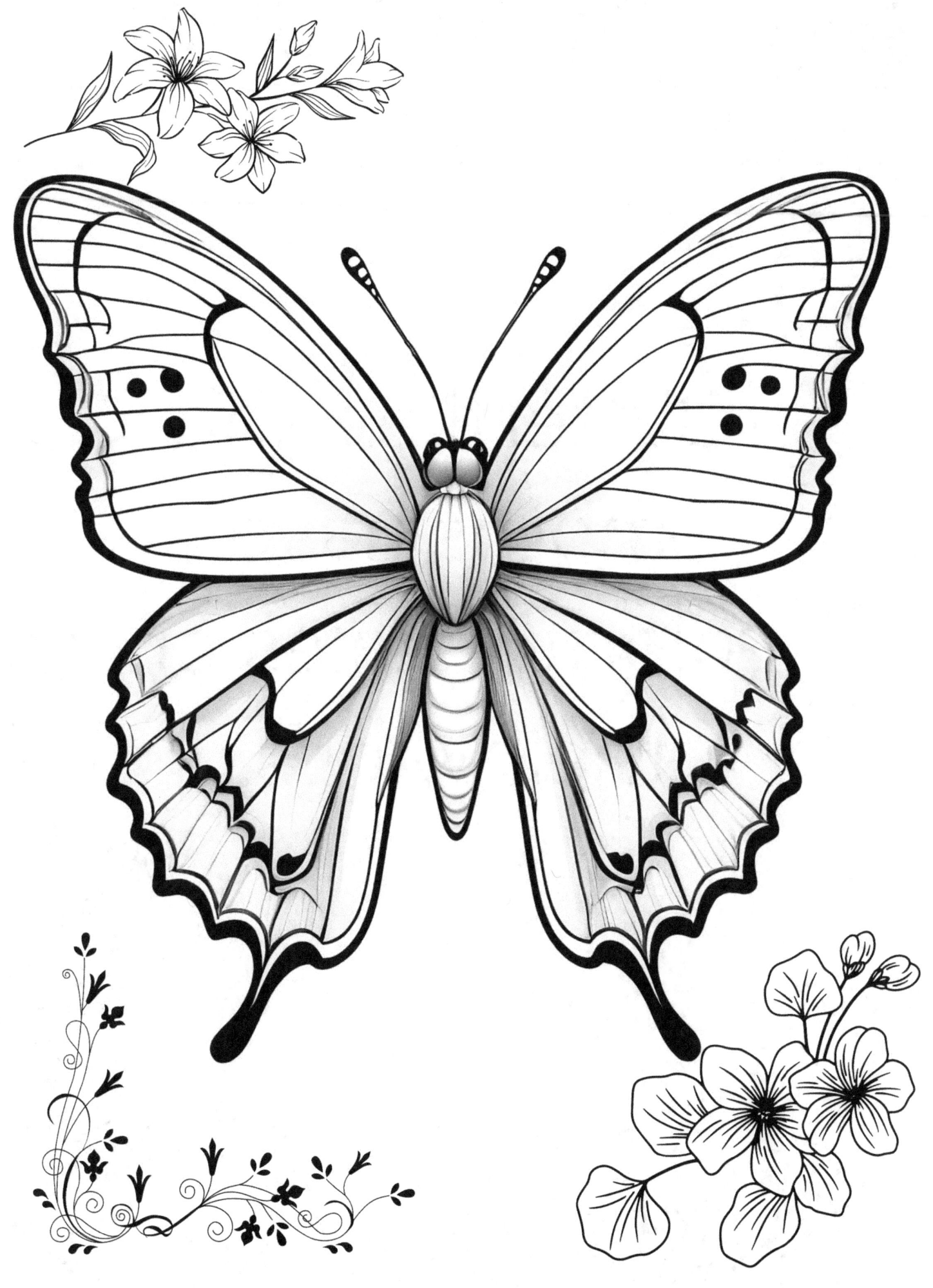

Butterflies and moths have colorful scales on their wings.

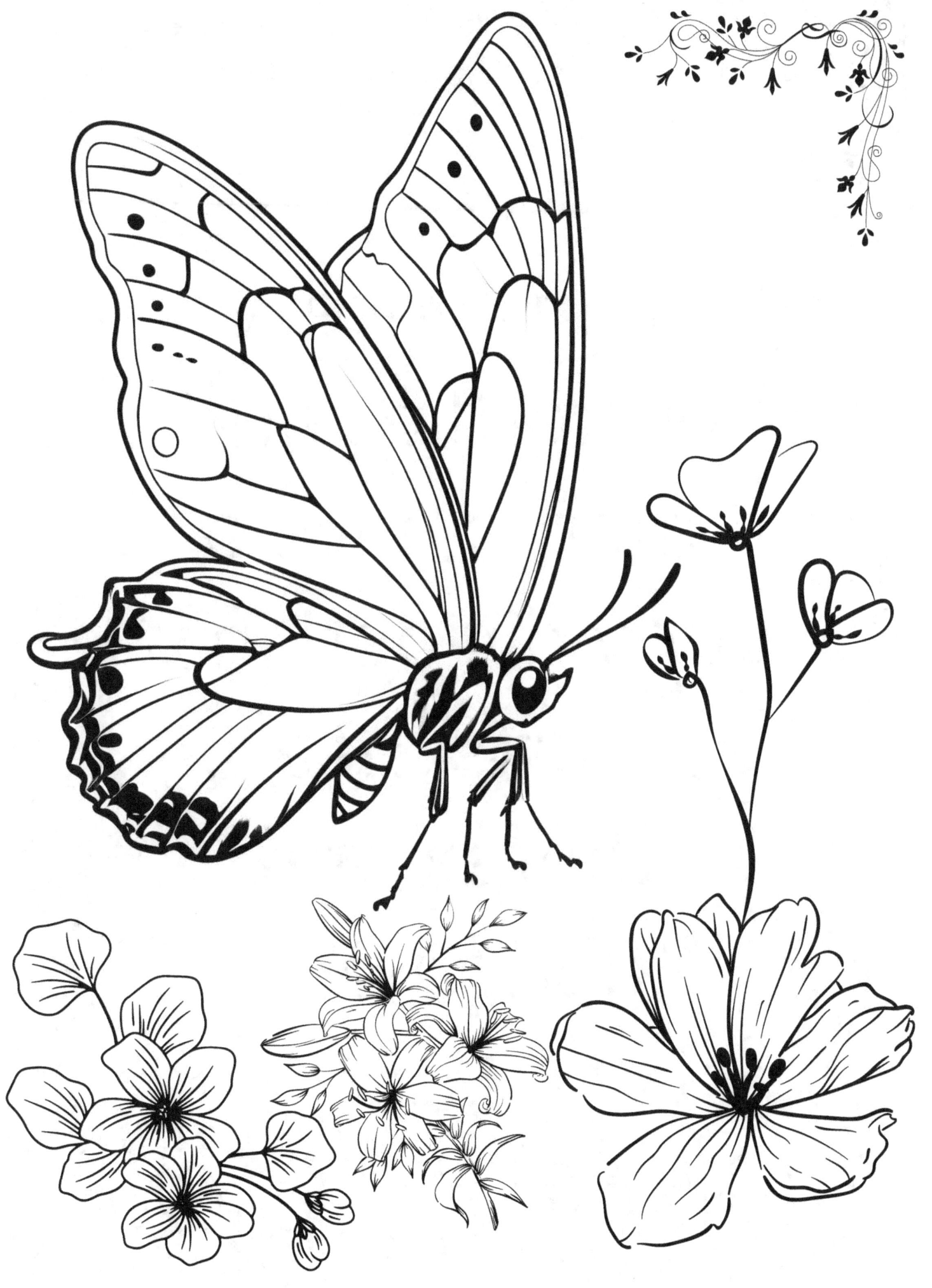

Like all insects, butterflies and moths have a body divided into 3 parts: head, thorax and abdomen.

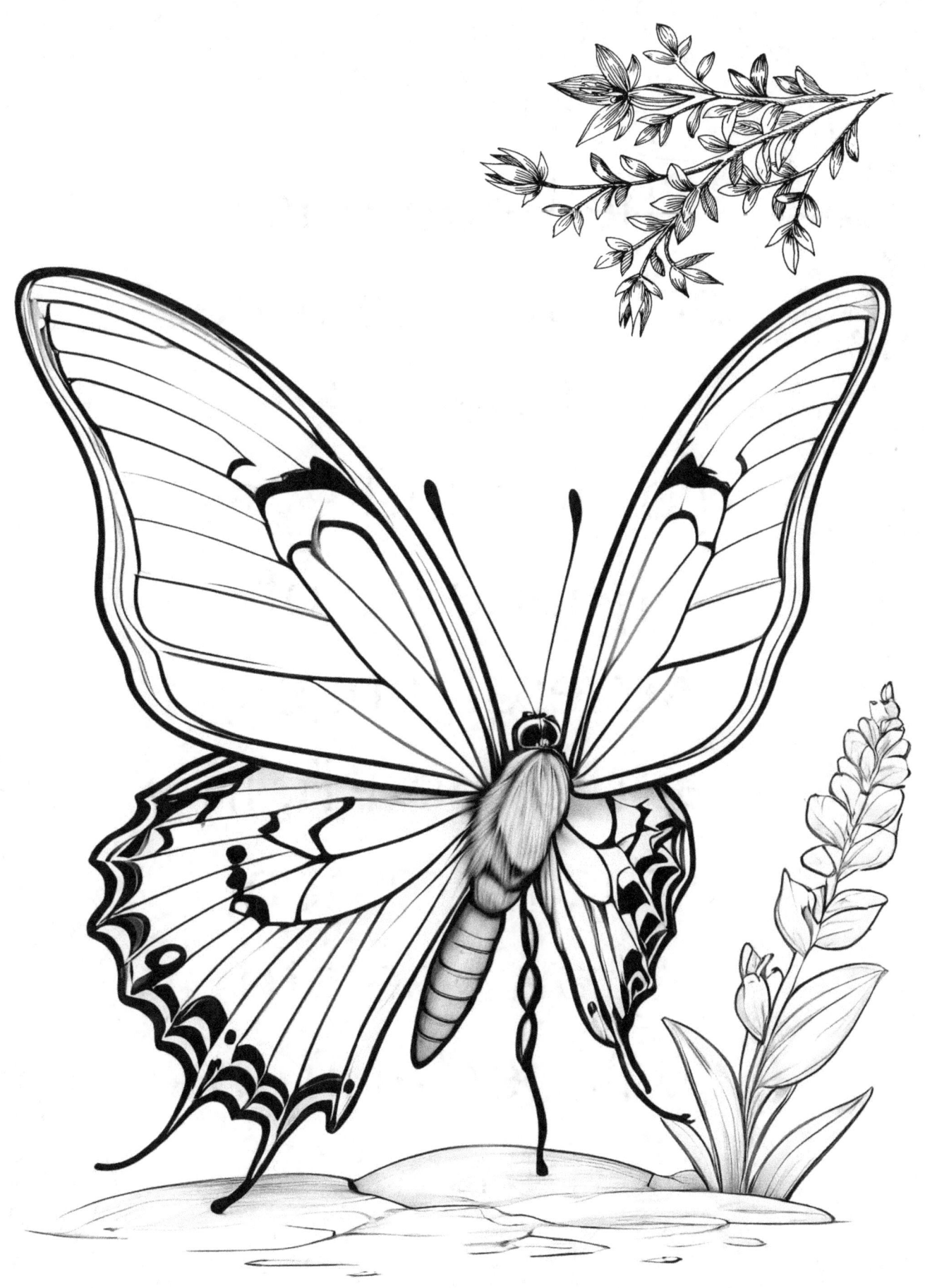

The head has 1 pair of antennae, 1 pair of compound eyes (made up of several lenses) and a mouth, in the form of a straw used to suck nectar from flowers.

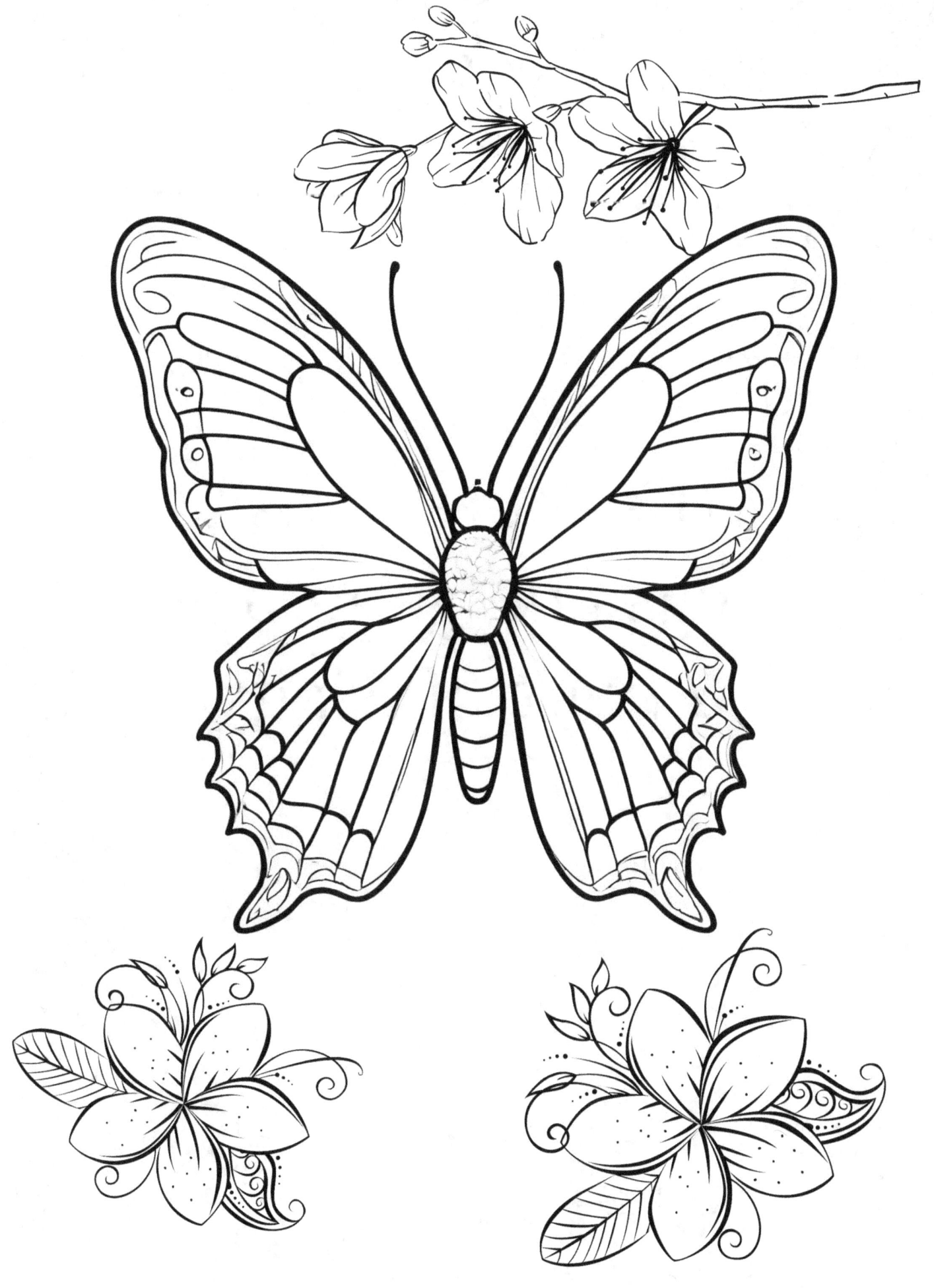

The thorax has 6 legs and generally 2 pairs of wings.

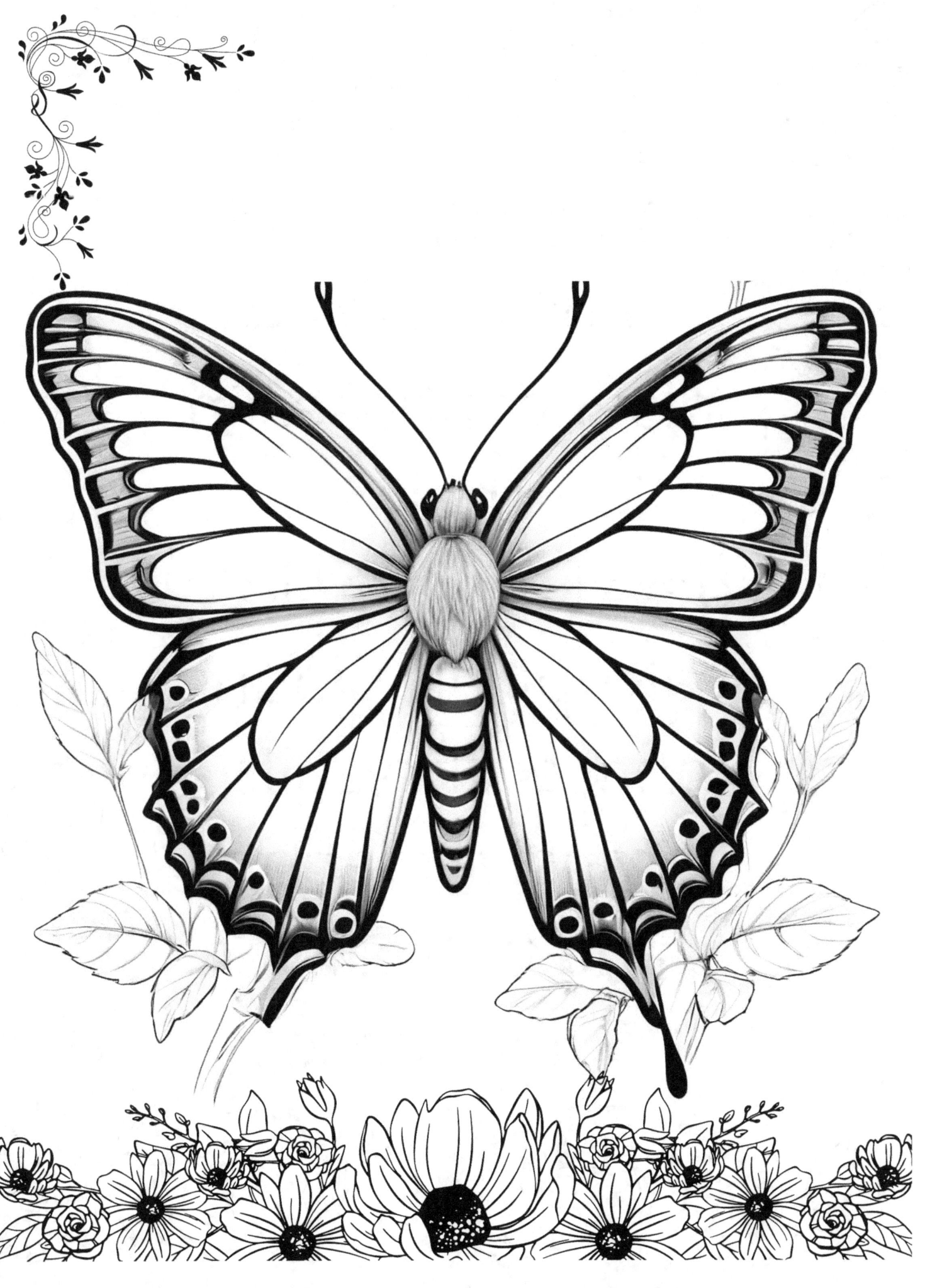

Butterflies and moths have 4 distinct phases in their development: egg, caterpillar - young phase, chrysalis - transformation and butterfly - adult phase.

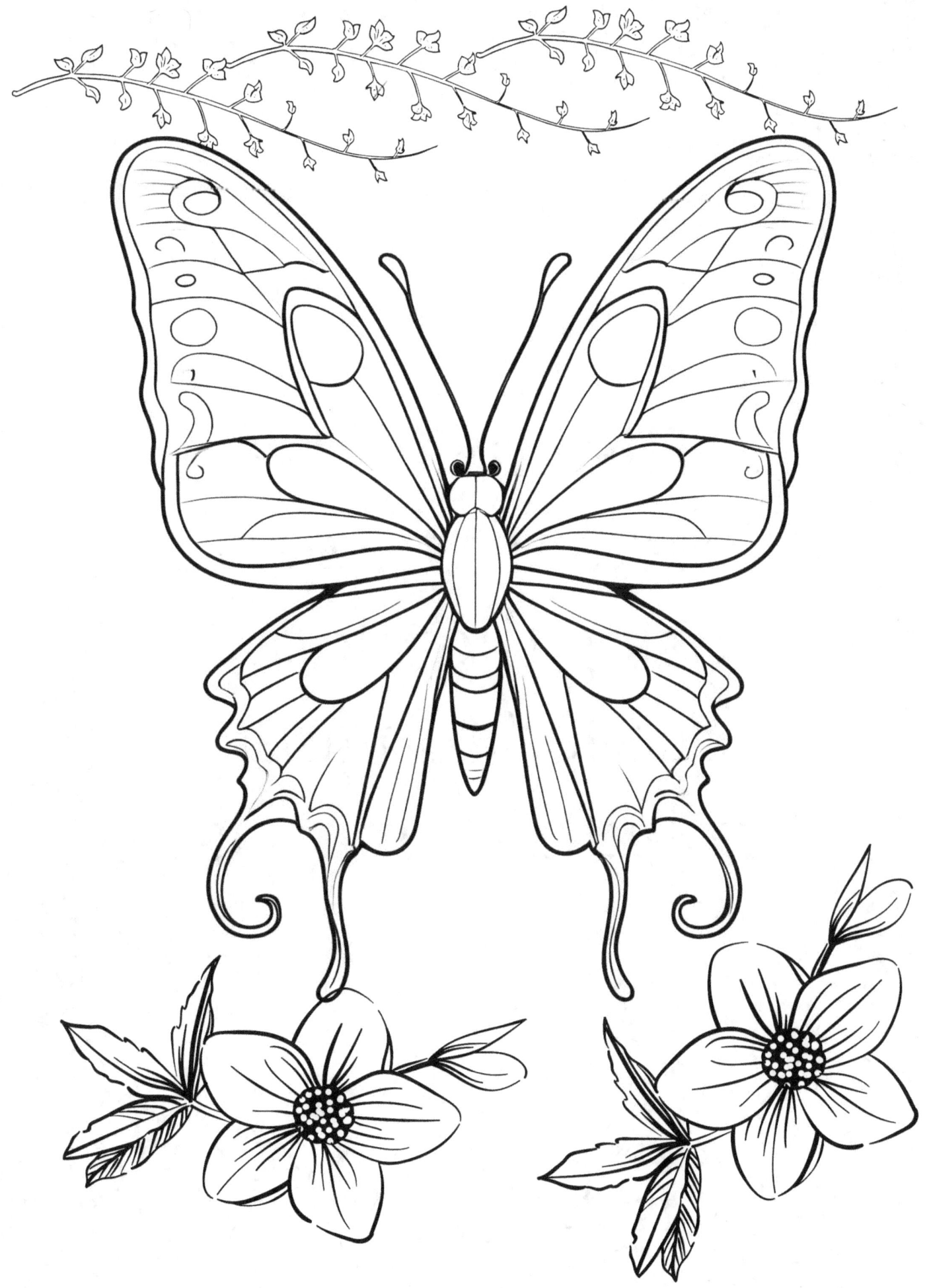

They taste the
nectar of flowers
using their long,
coiled tongue
called a proboscis.

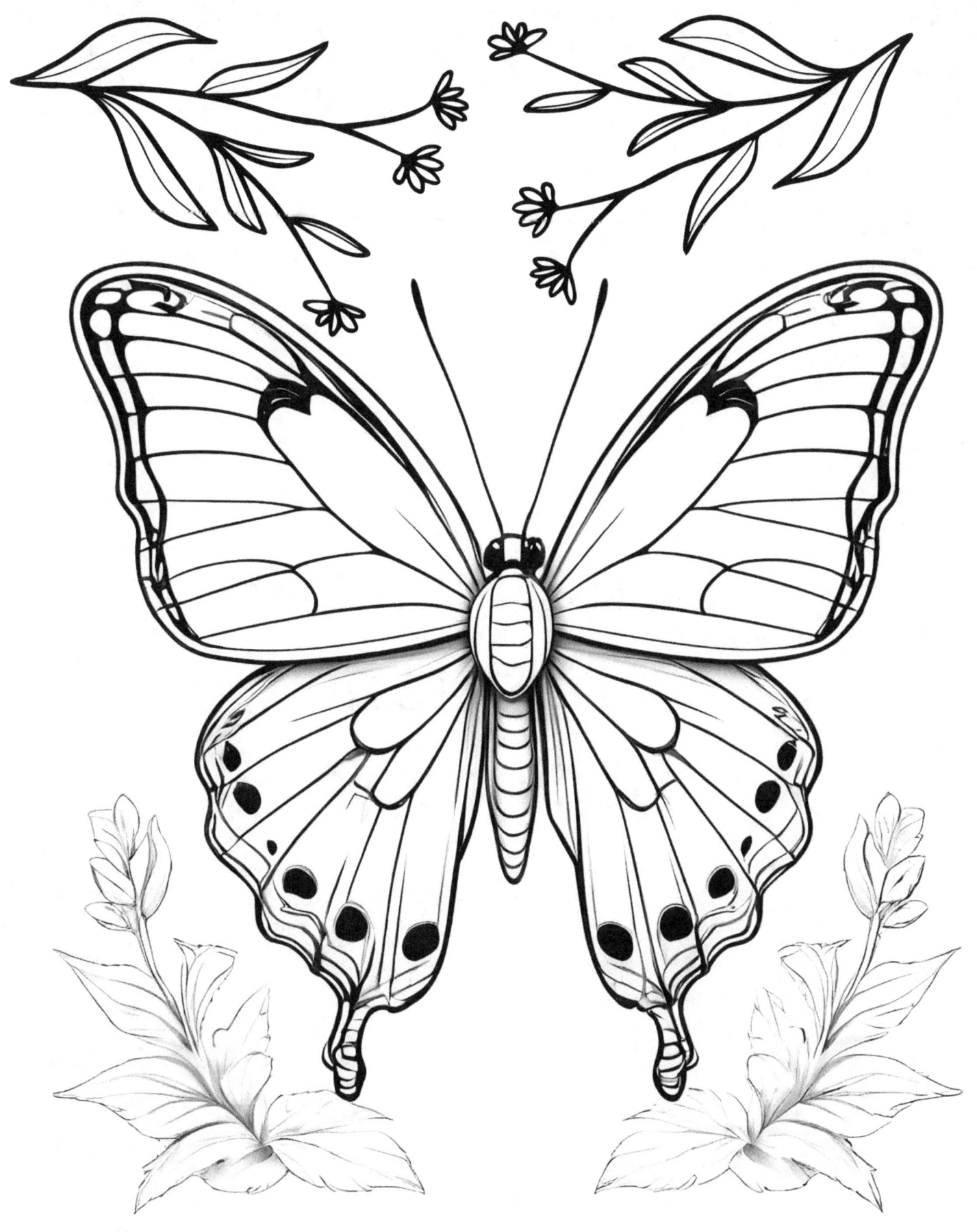

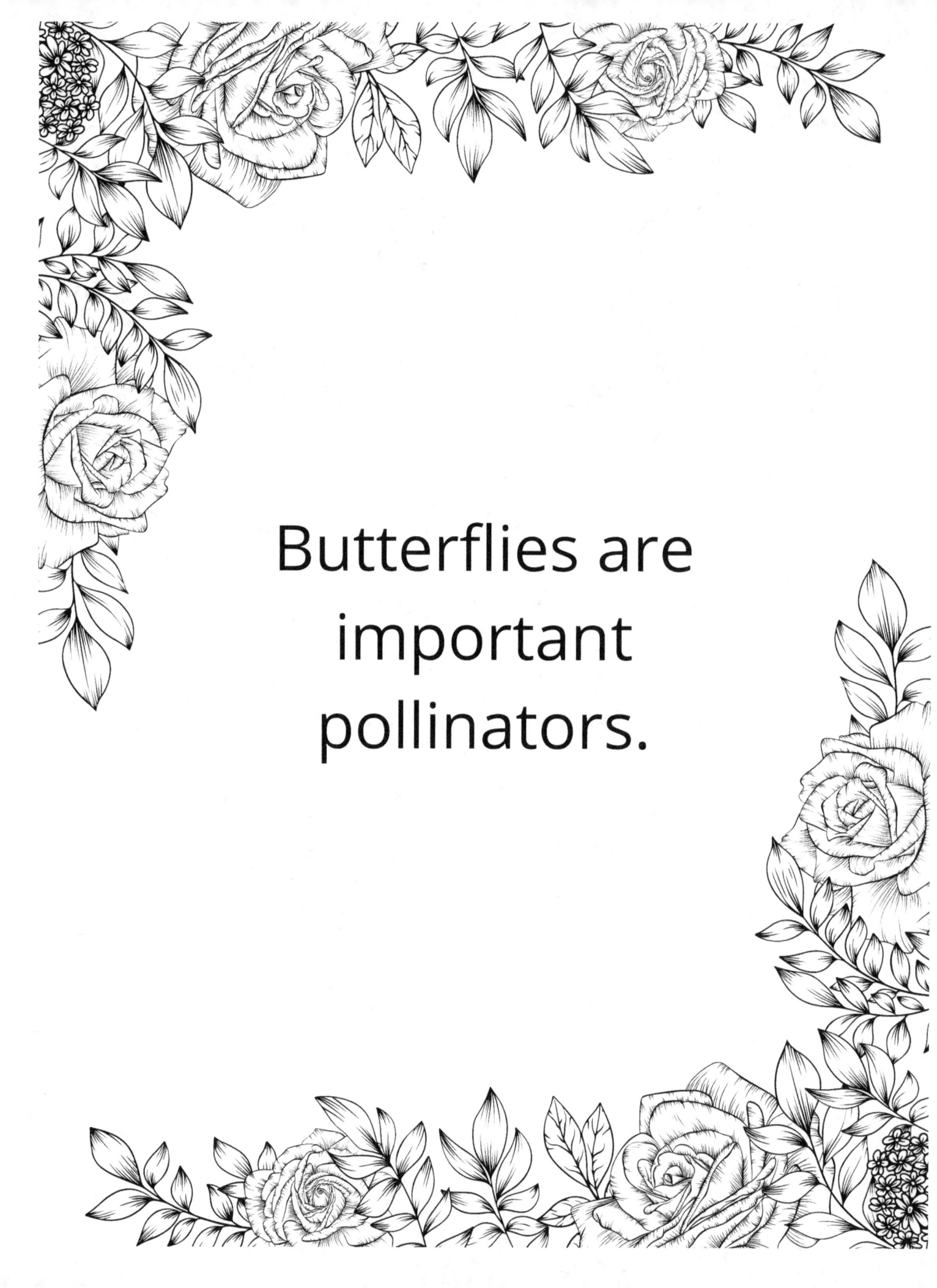

Butterflies are important pollinators.

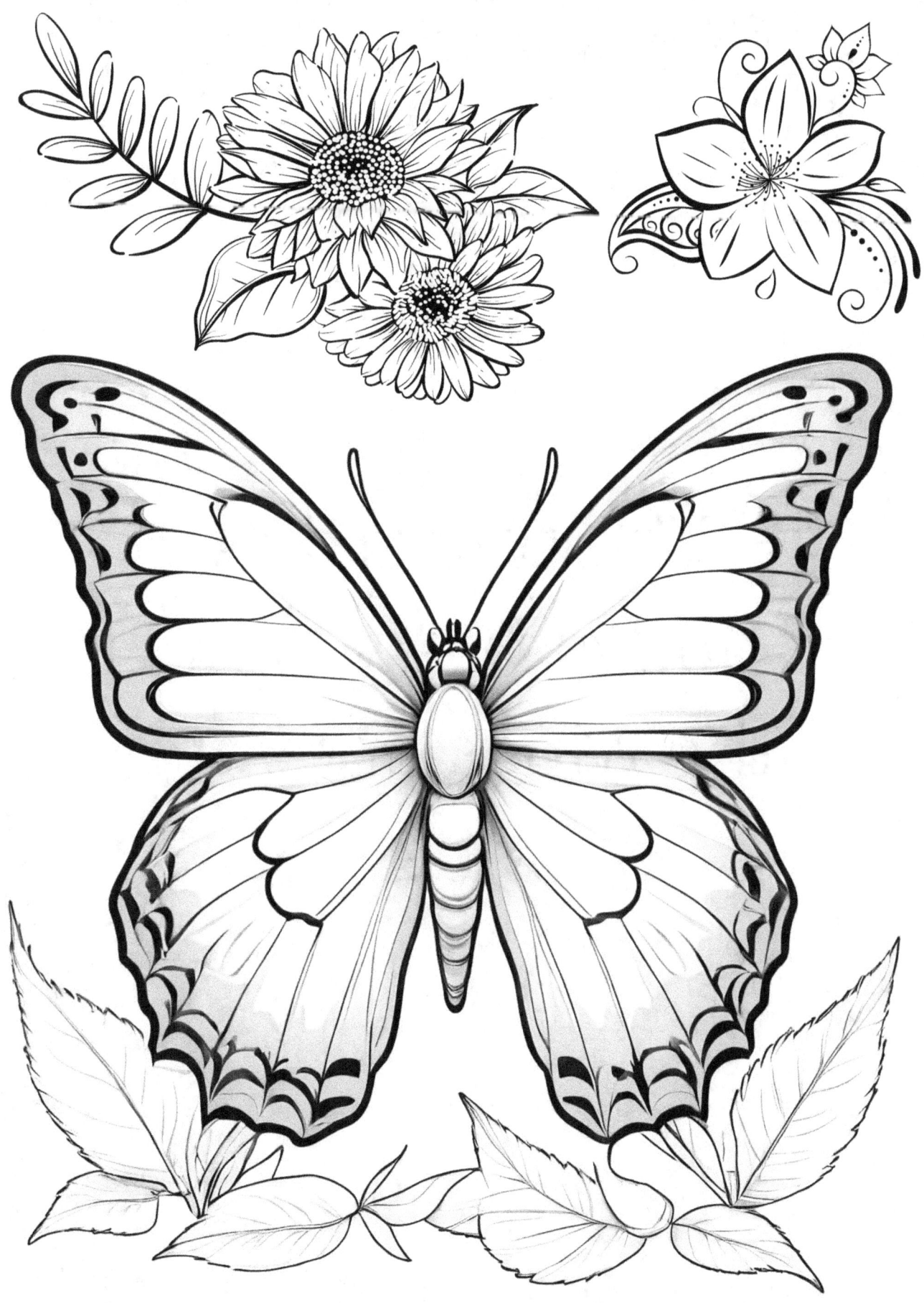

The butterfly's body is very light, the wings are very wide.

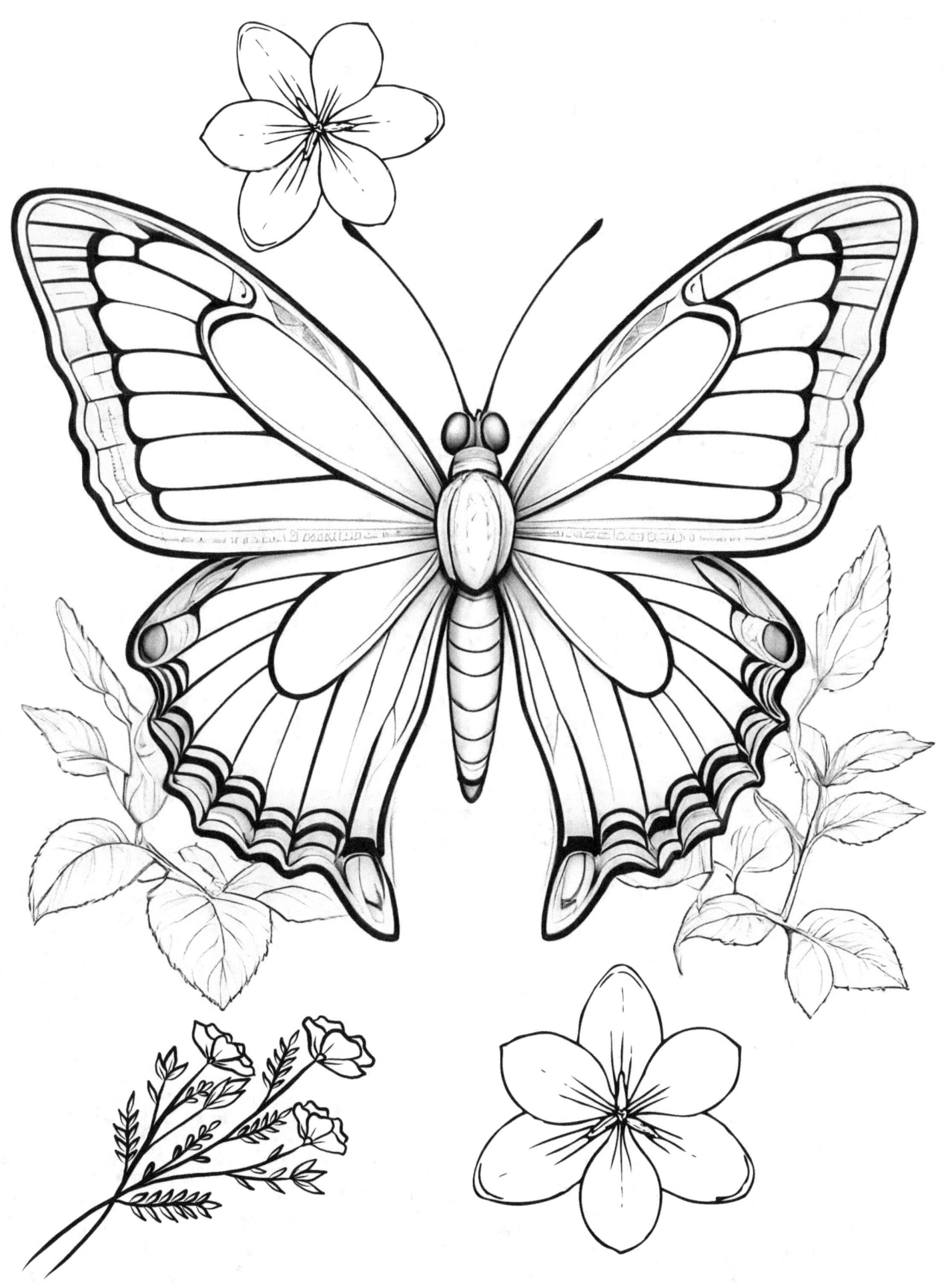

Butterflies exist in all parts of the world, with the exception of glacial regions.

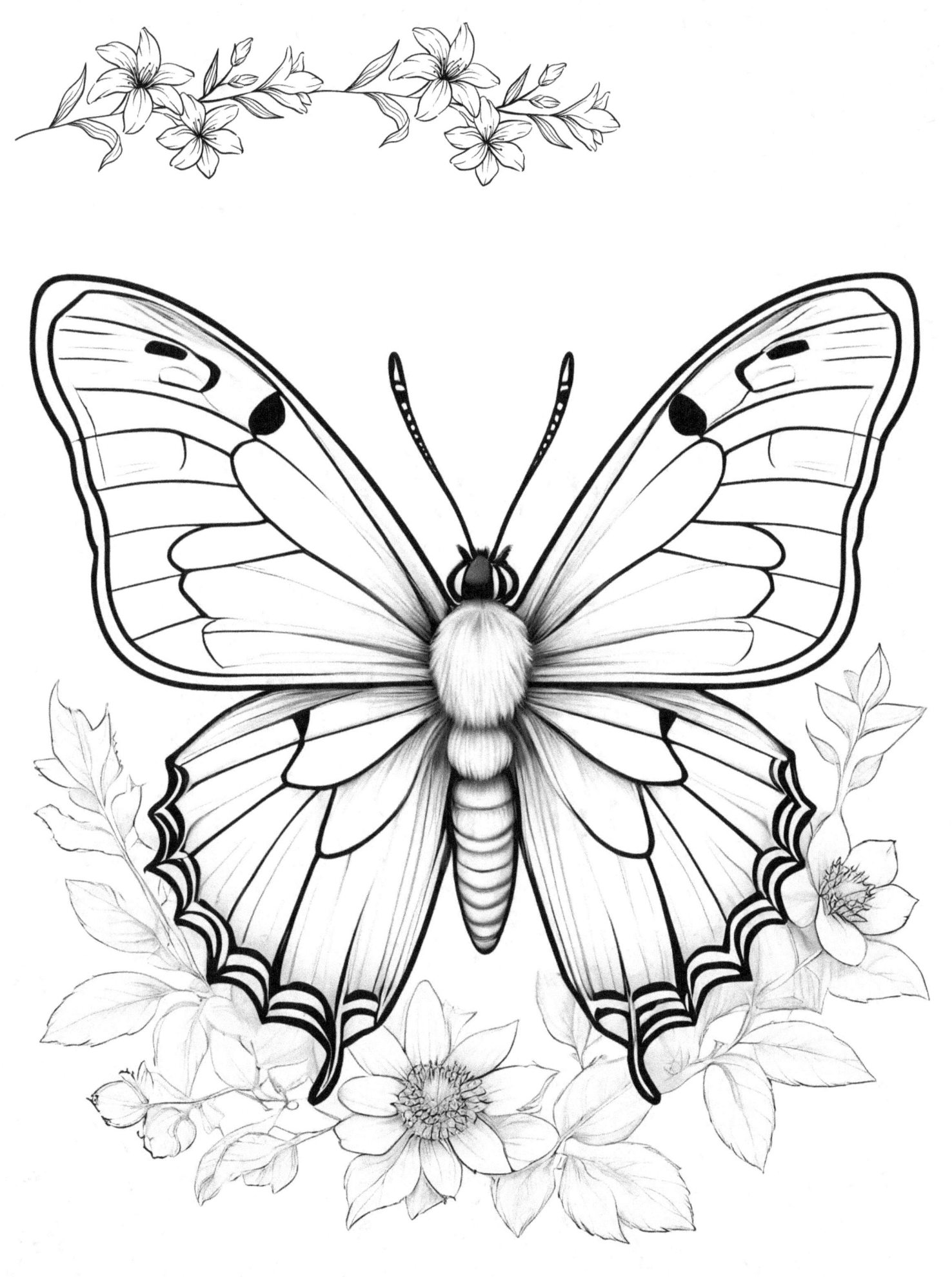

Almost all butterfly species are active during the day.

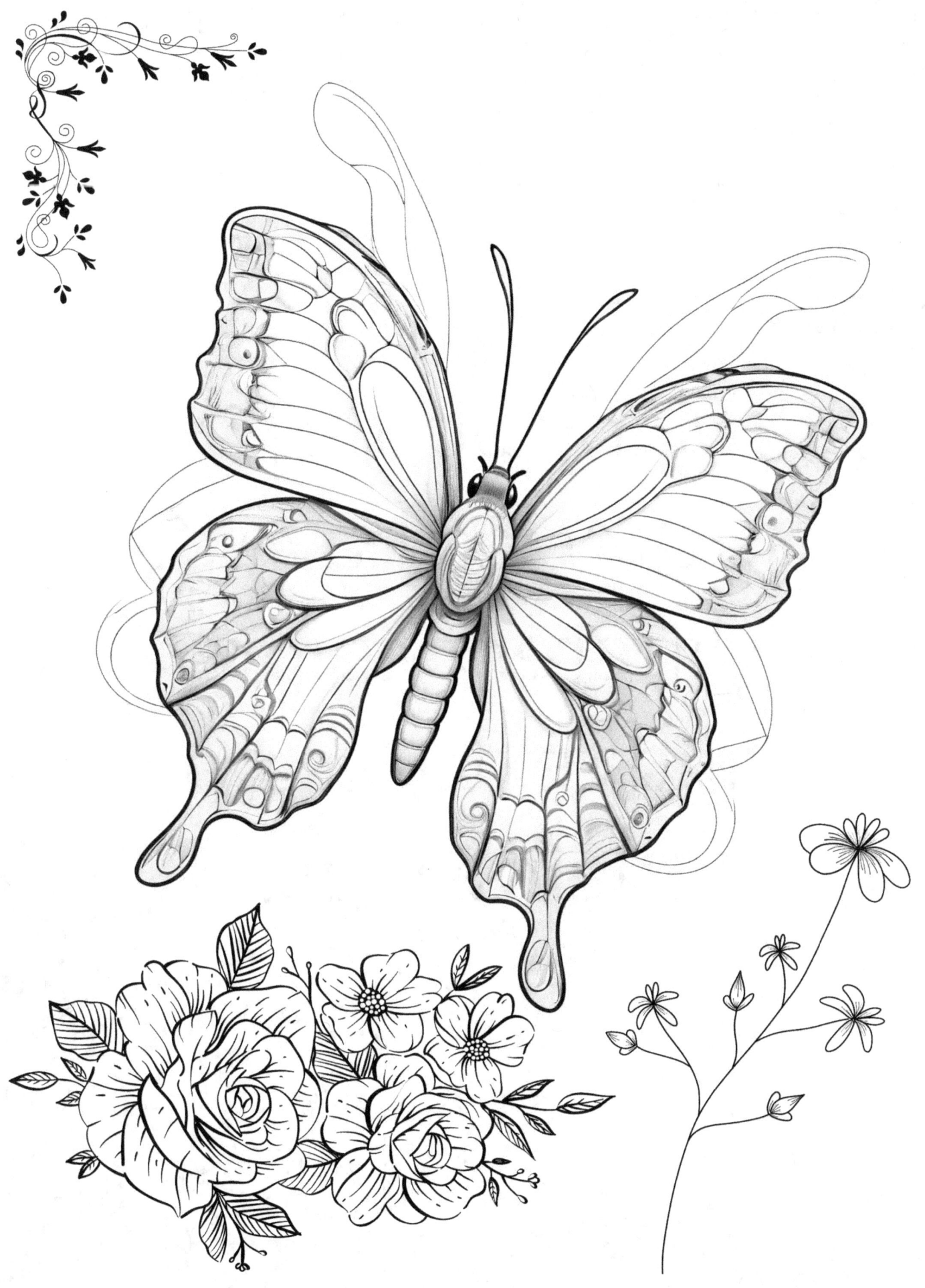

Many butterfly species have different colors and textures on their wings.

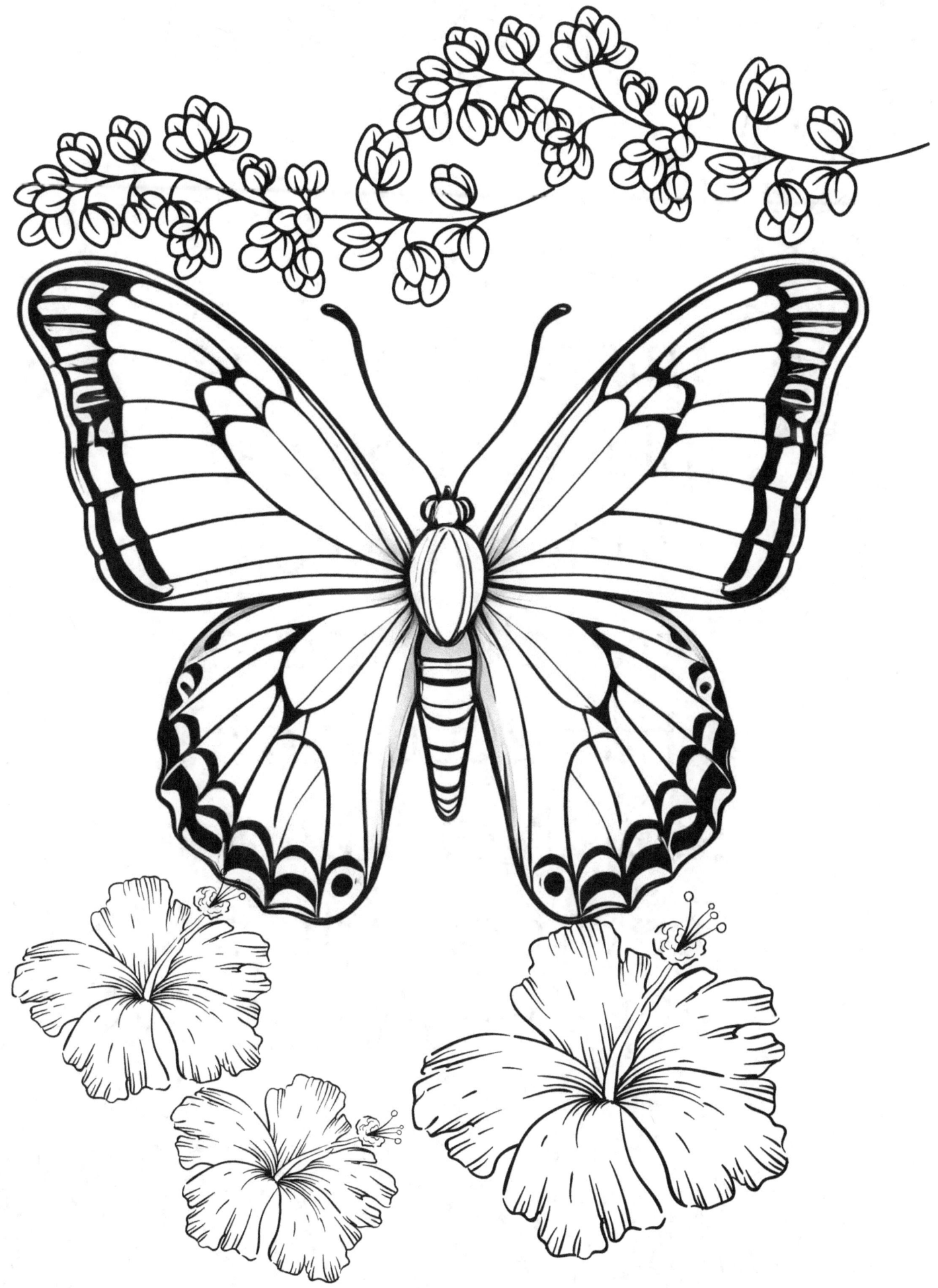

Some species migrate to more pleasant places, during the cold, traveling more than 2000 km in search of a better environment for their survival.

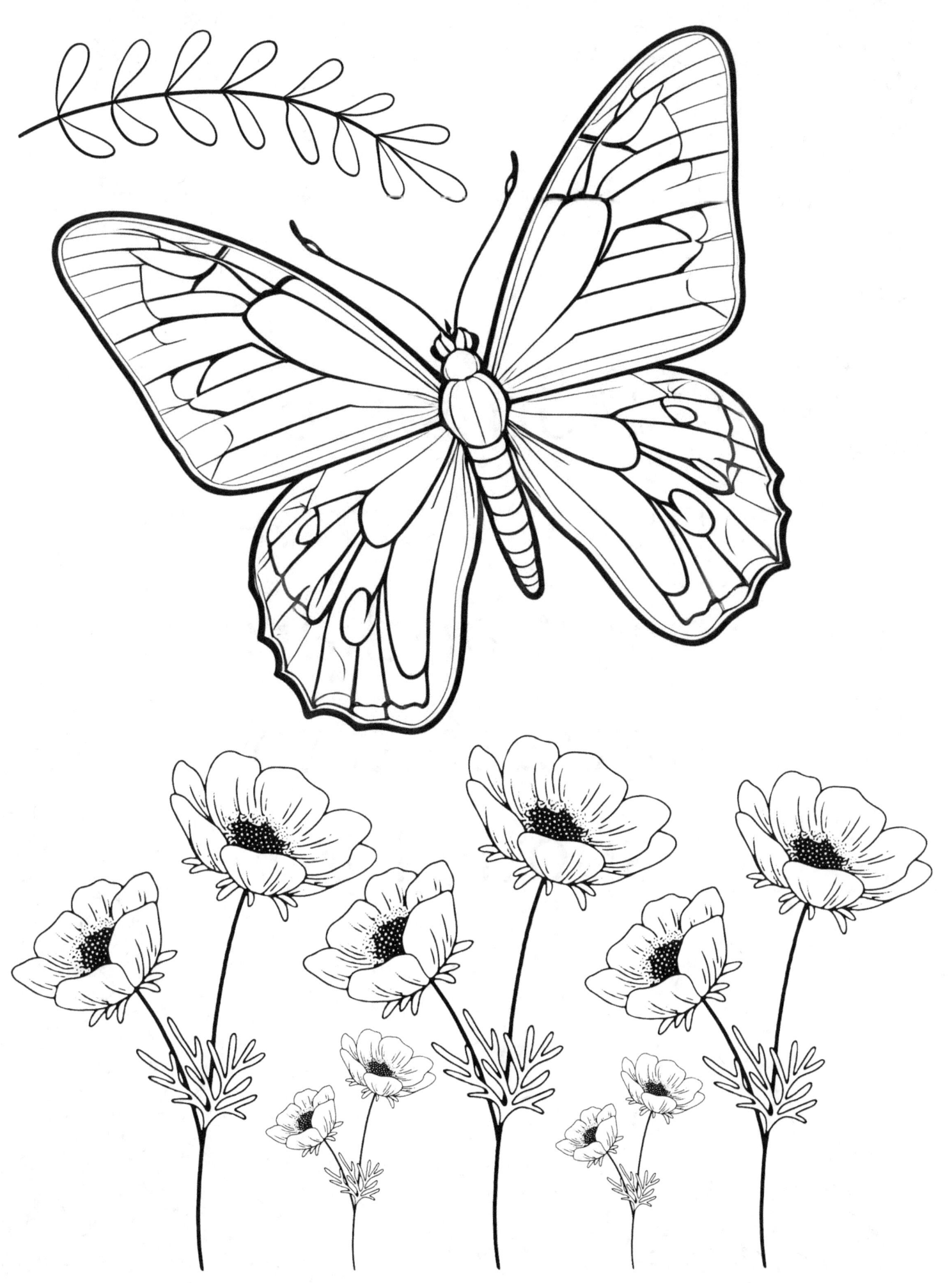

Moths are generally active at night and are attracted to spotlights.

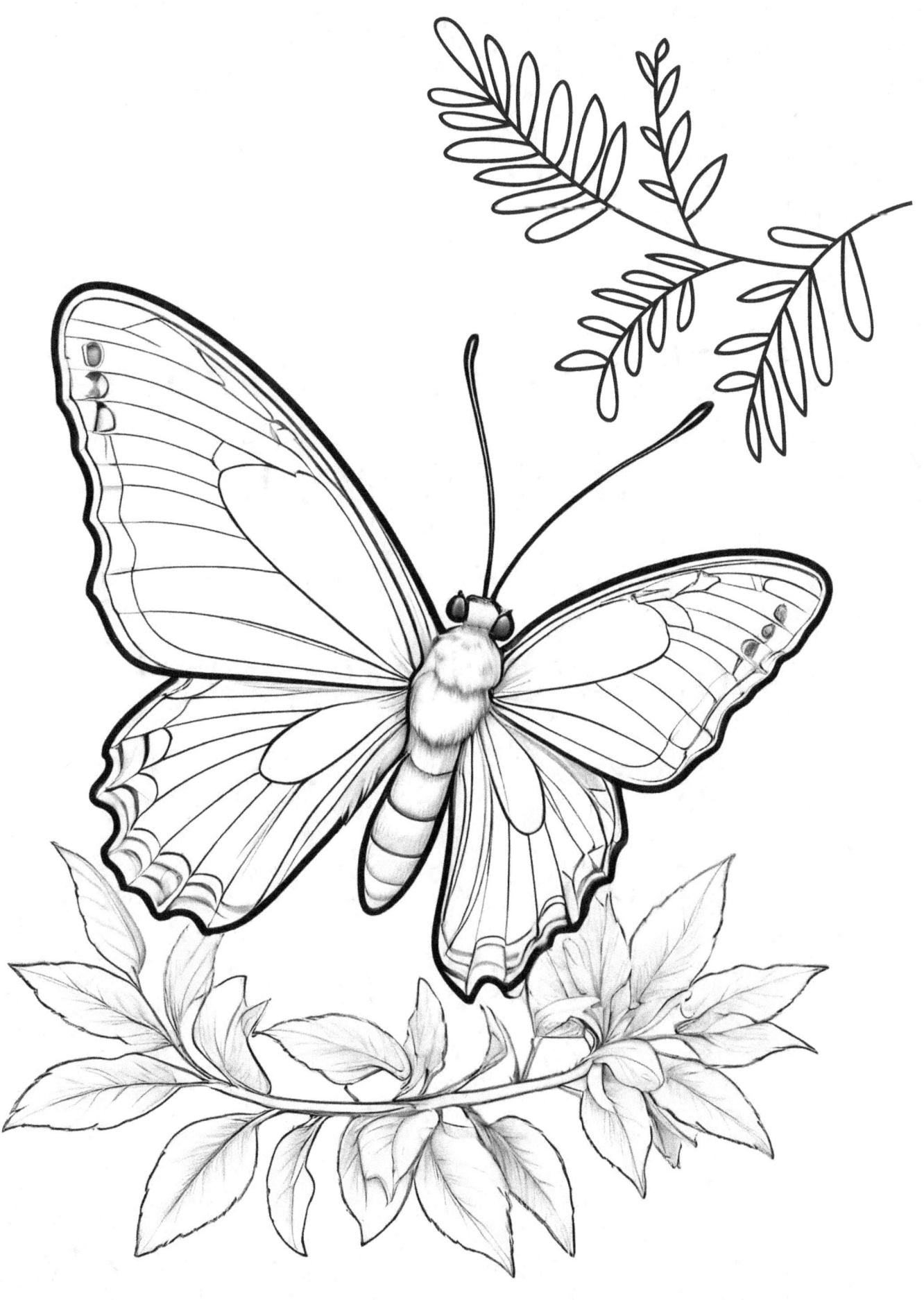

Chrysalis form. At this stage, it remains hanging, upside down, and some time later it transforms into an adult insect.

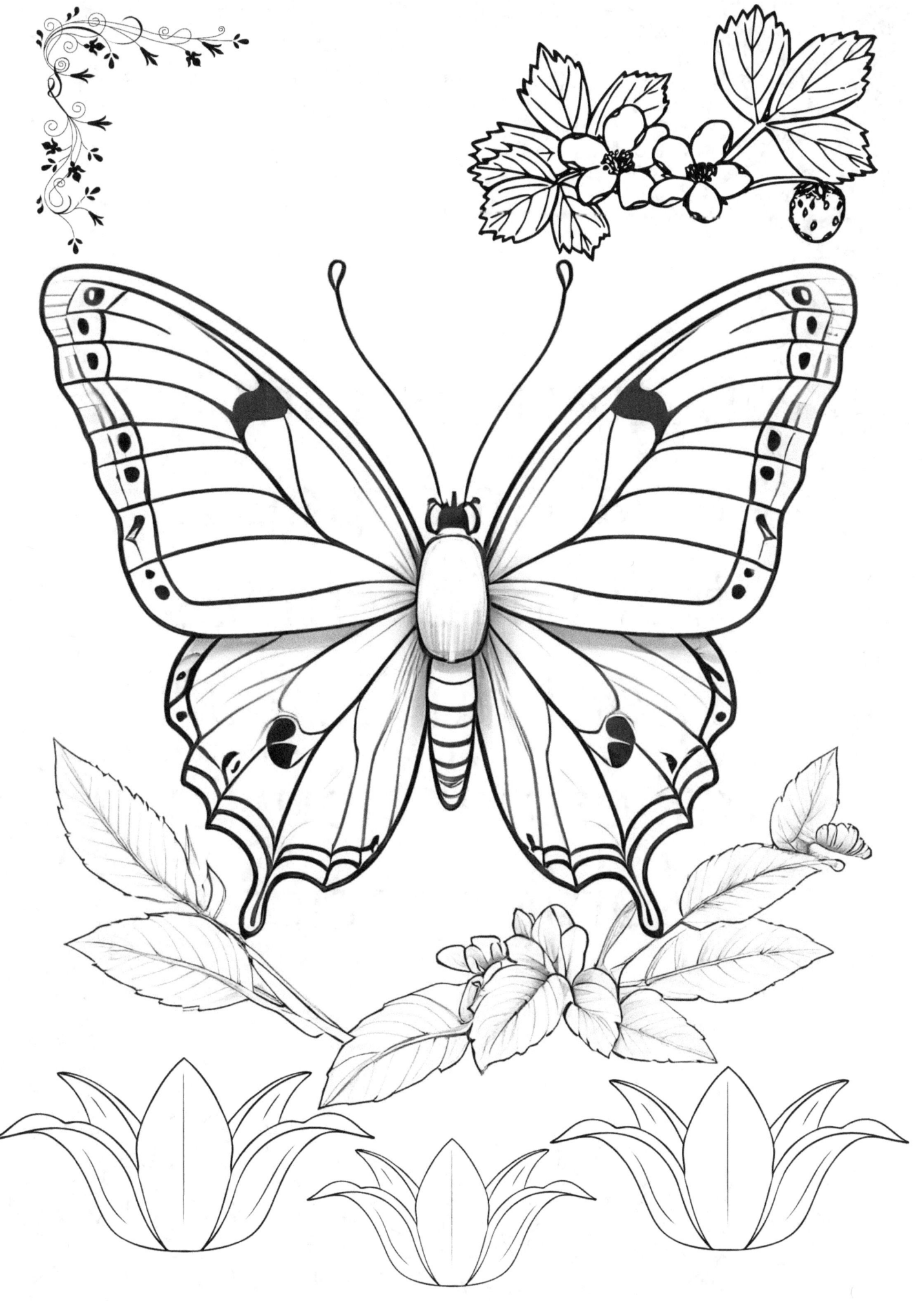

Butterflies can fly at varying speeds, from a few miles per hour to 30 miles per hour in some species.

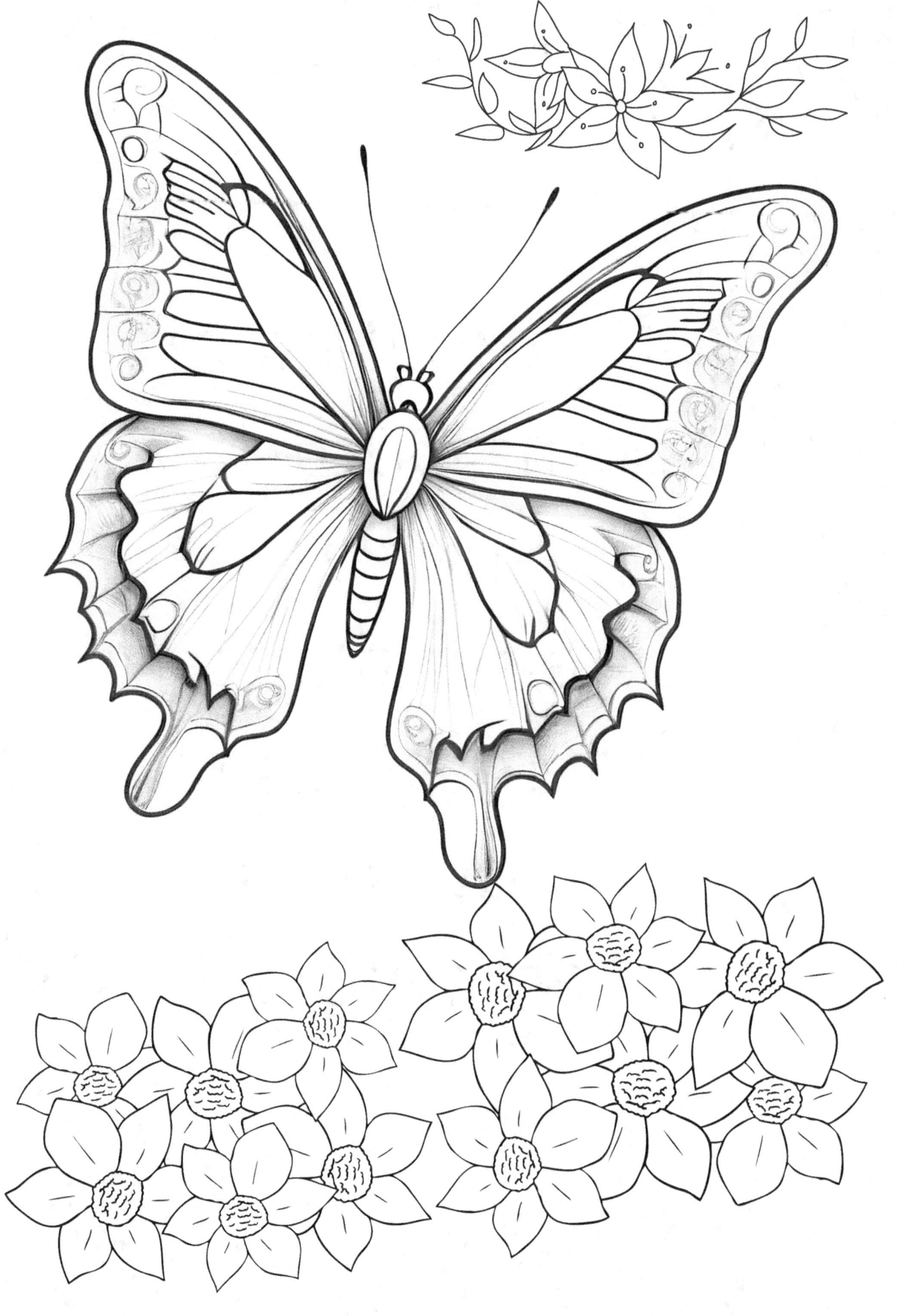

Caterpillars of some butterfly species camouflage themselves to hide from predators.

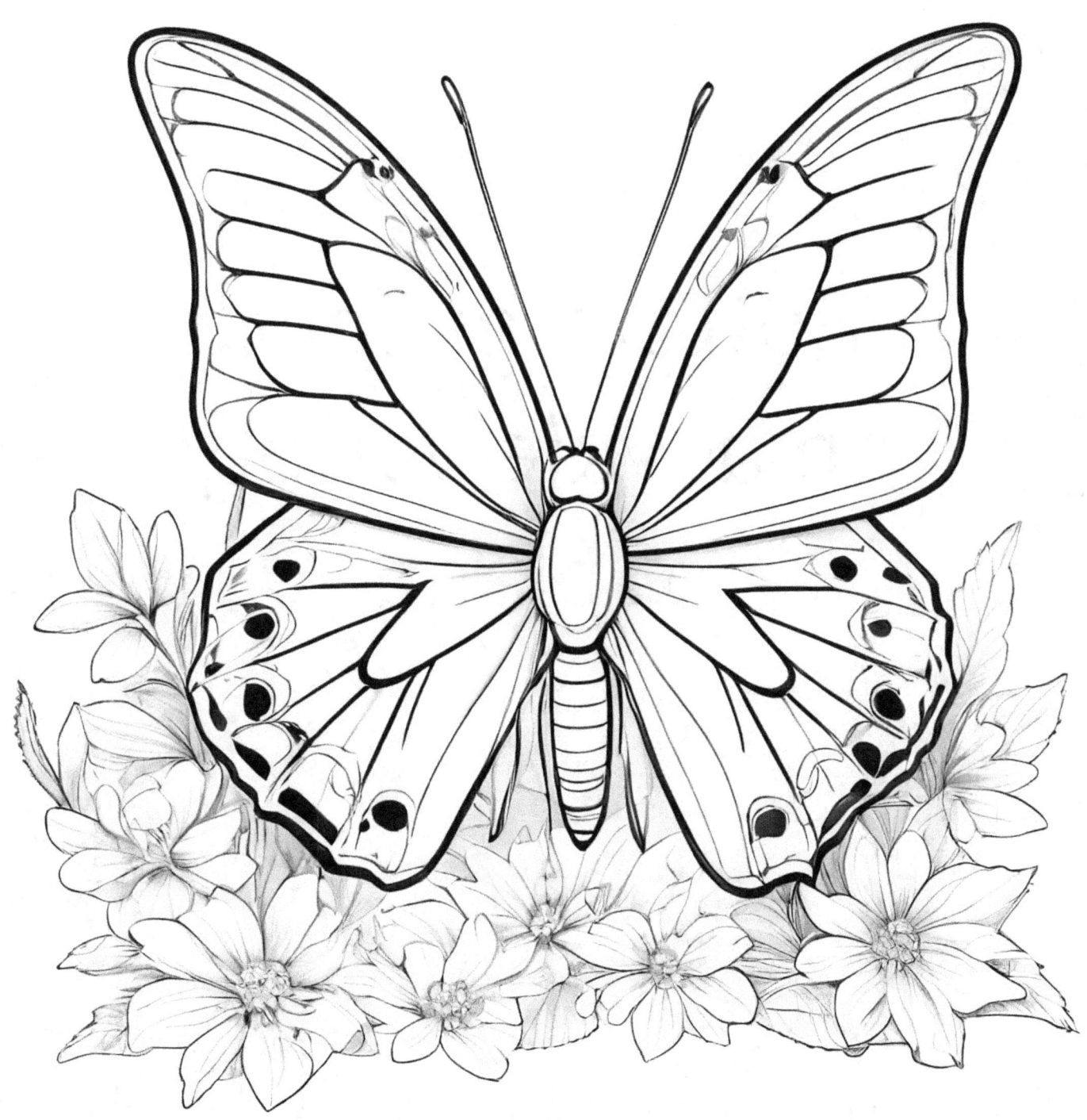

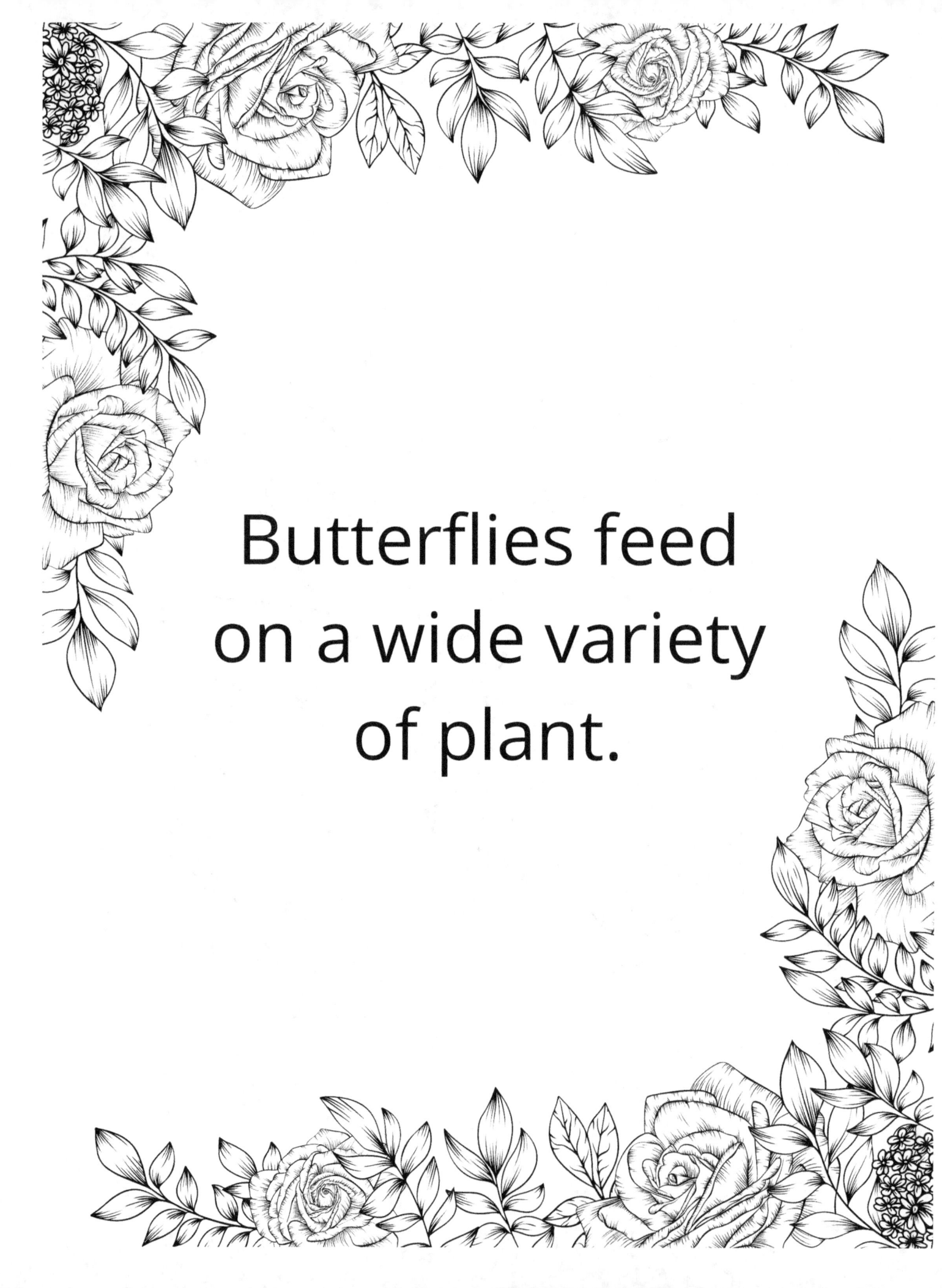

Butterflies feed on a wide variety of plant.

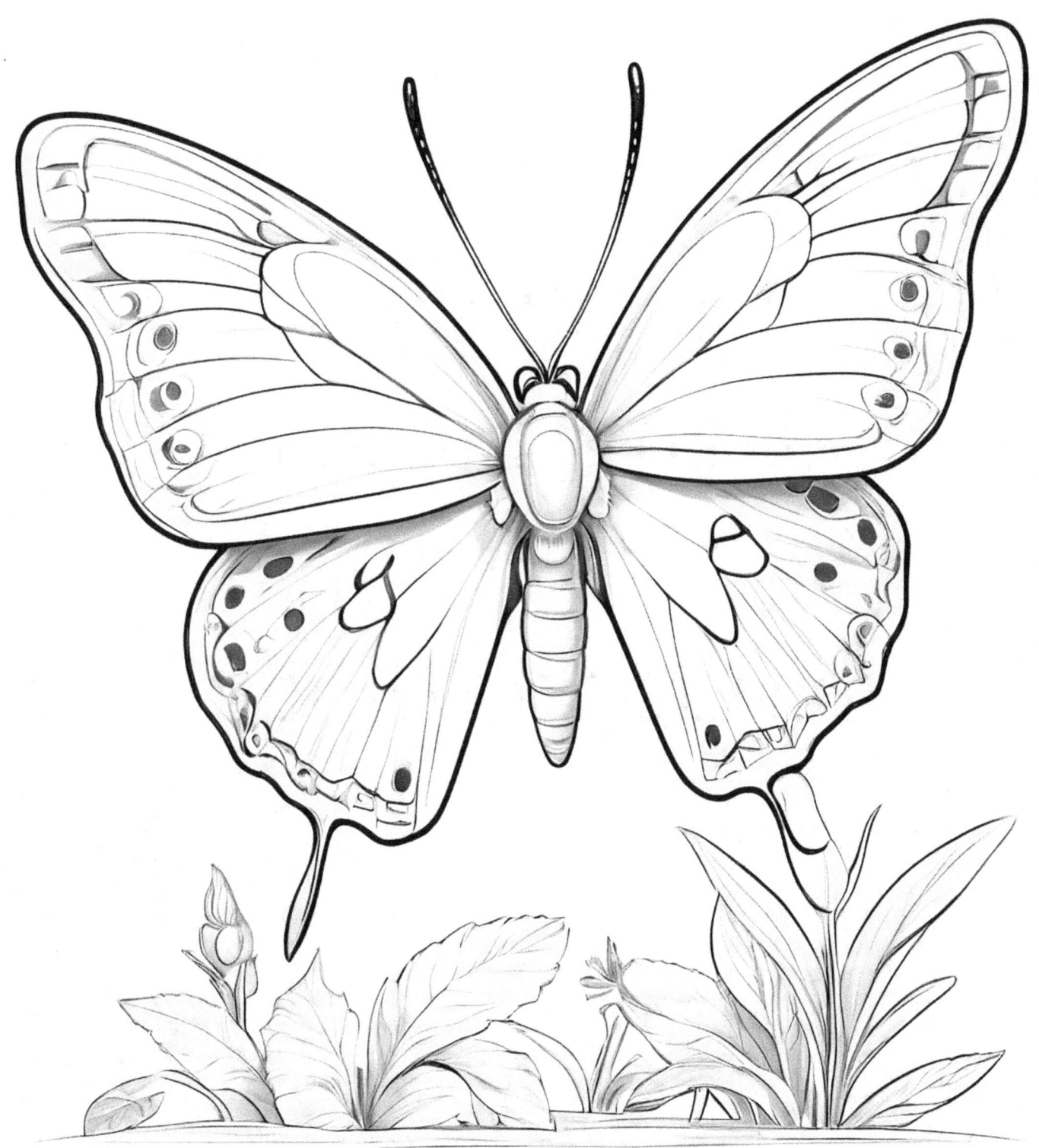

The study of butterflies is called lepidopterology.

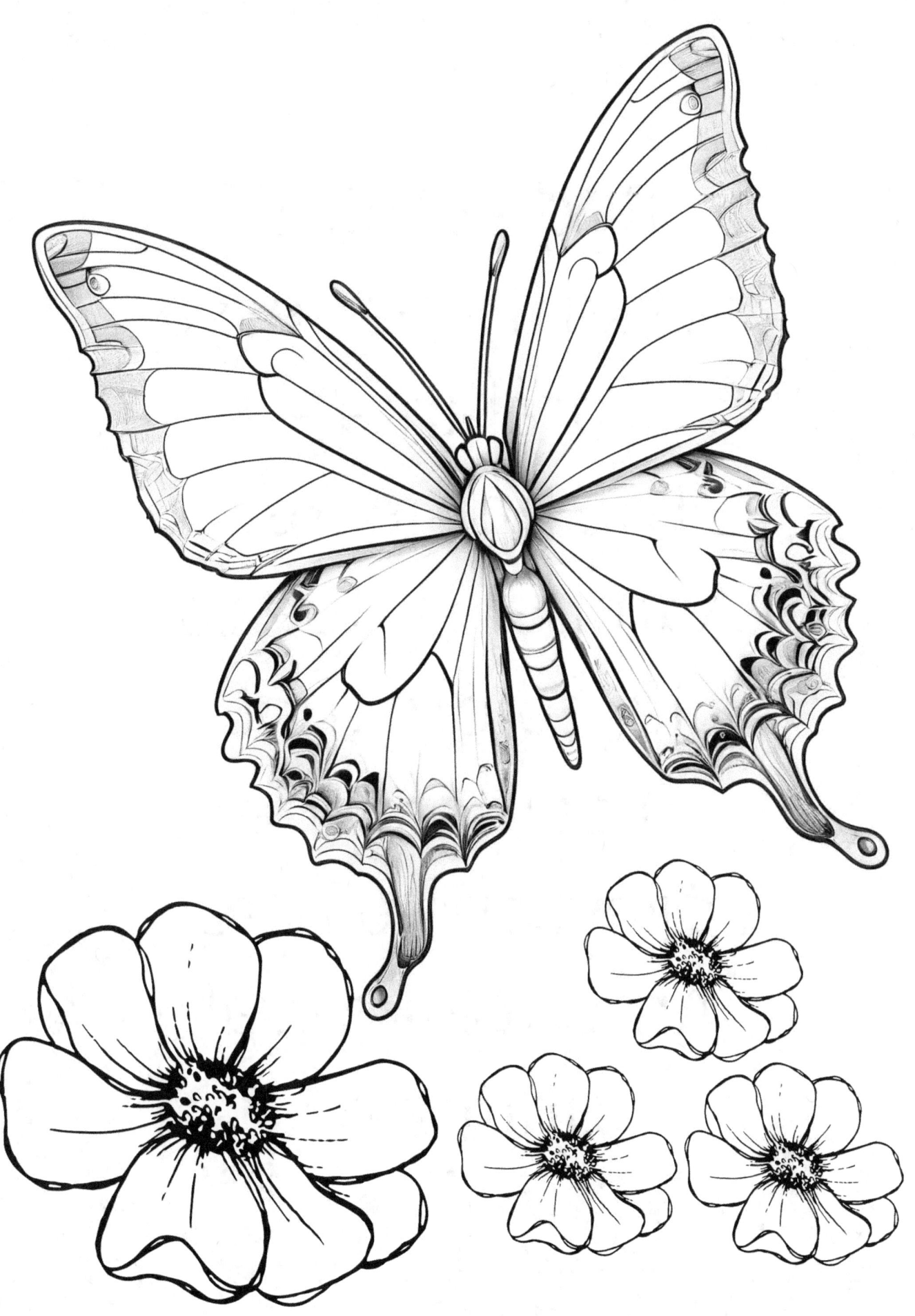

Red admiral butterfly (vanessa atalanta)
The name Red Admiral is due to its colors that resemble the chevrons of the American naval uniform.

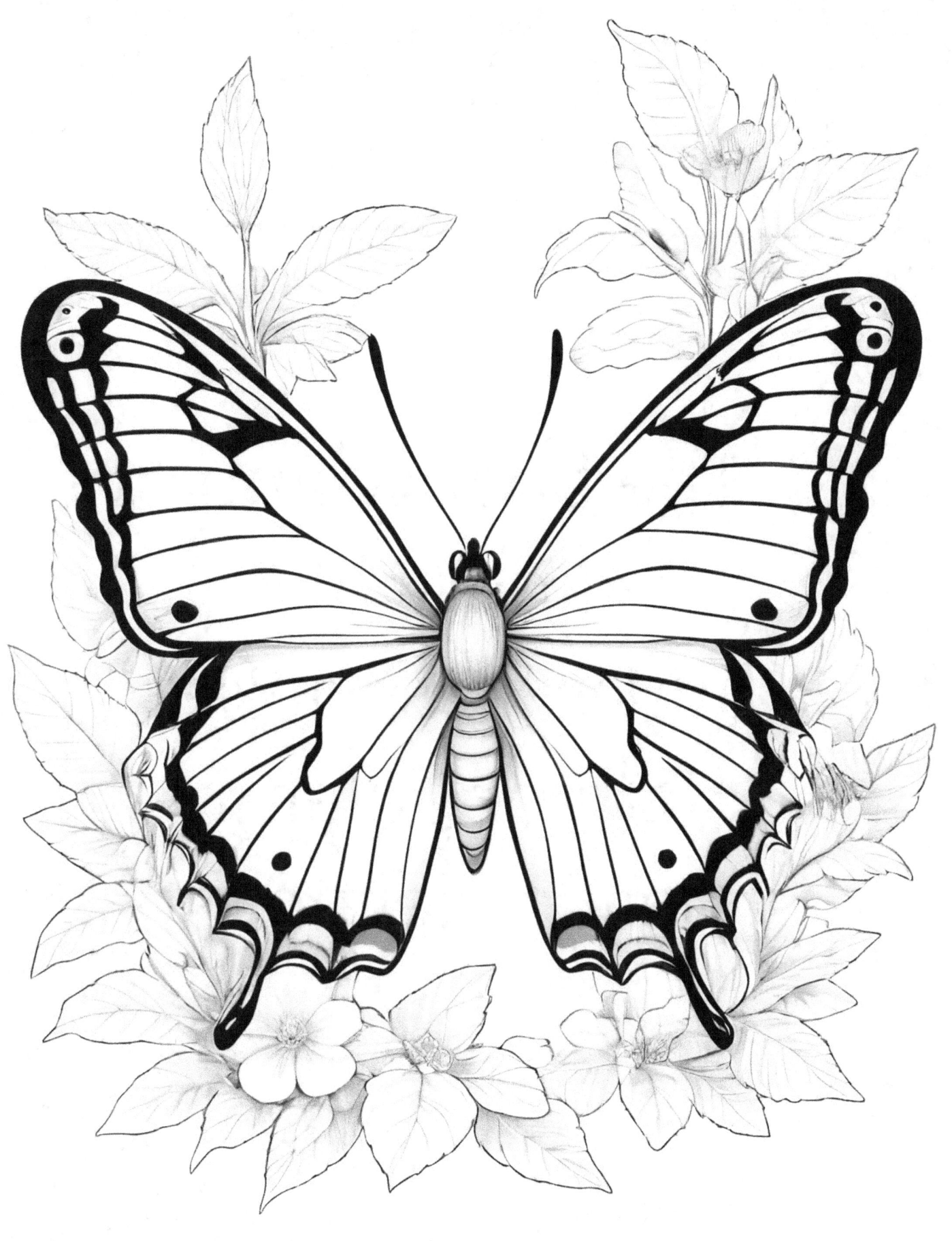

The beauty and variety of butterflies make them popular in insect collections.

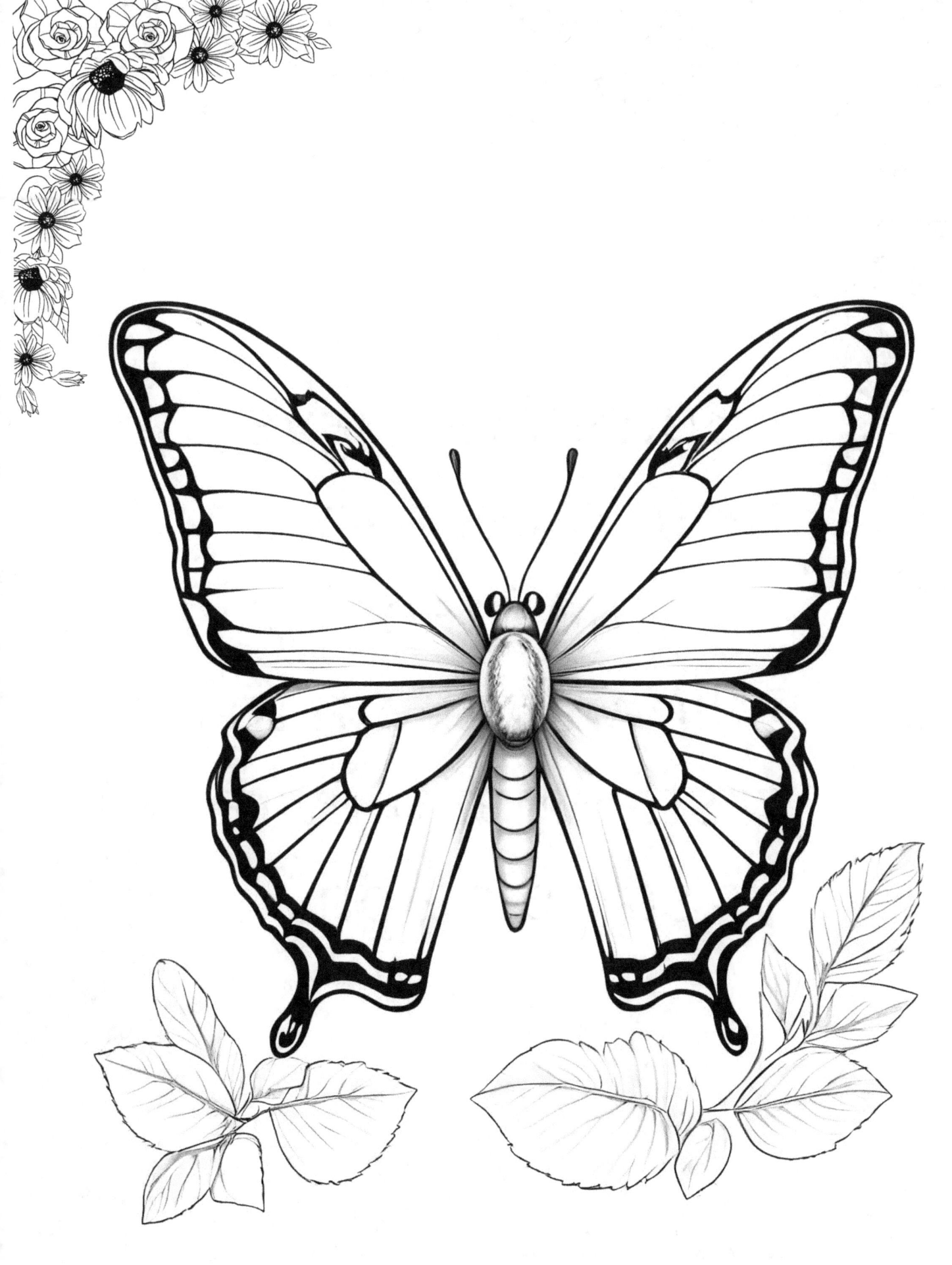

Butterflies have taste receptors on their feet, allowing them to taste what they're standing on.

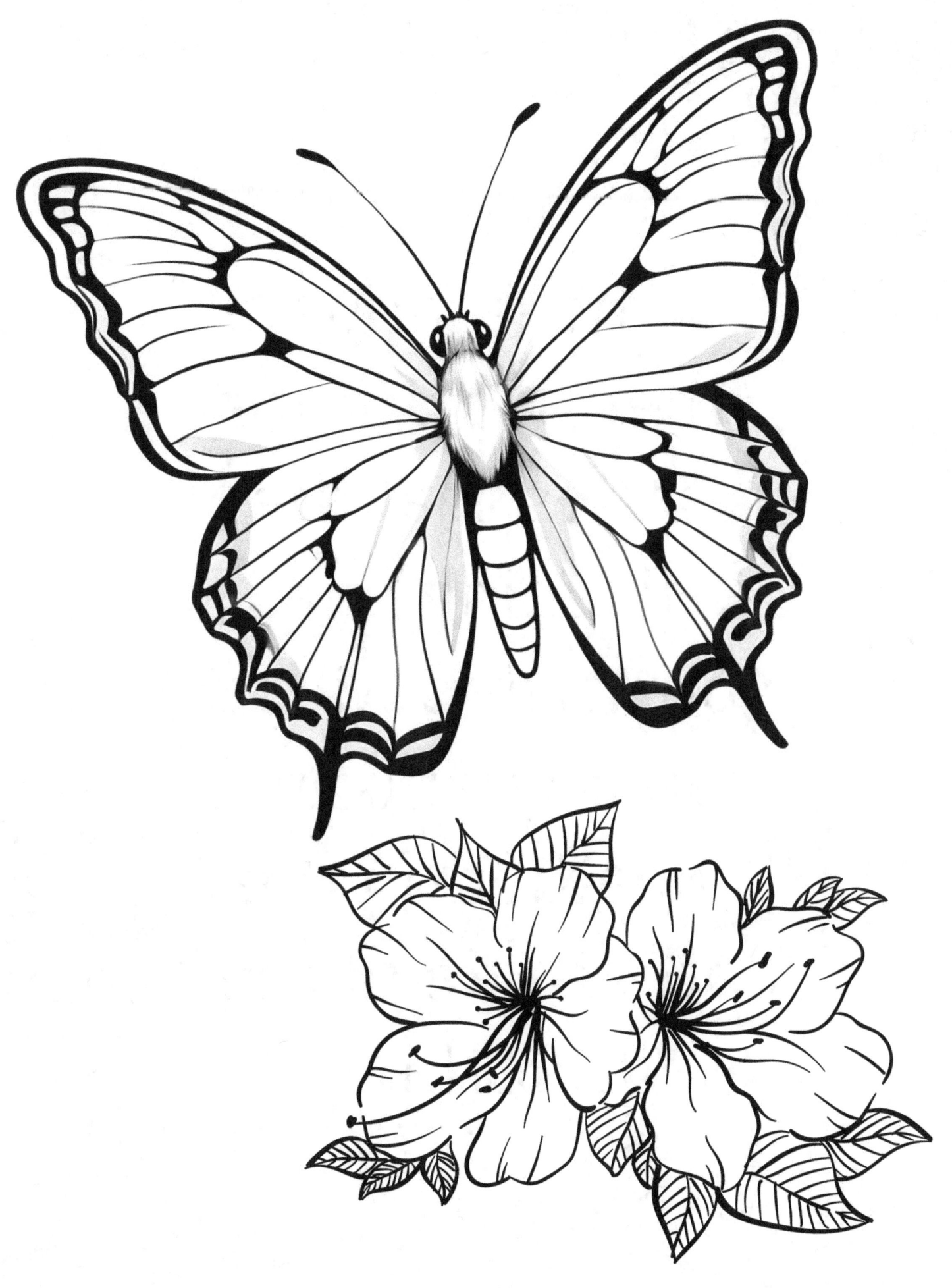

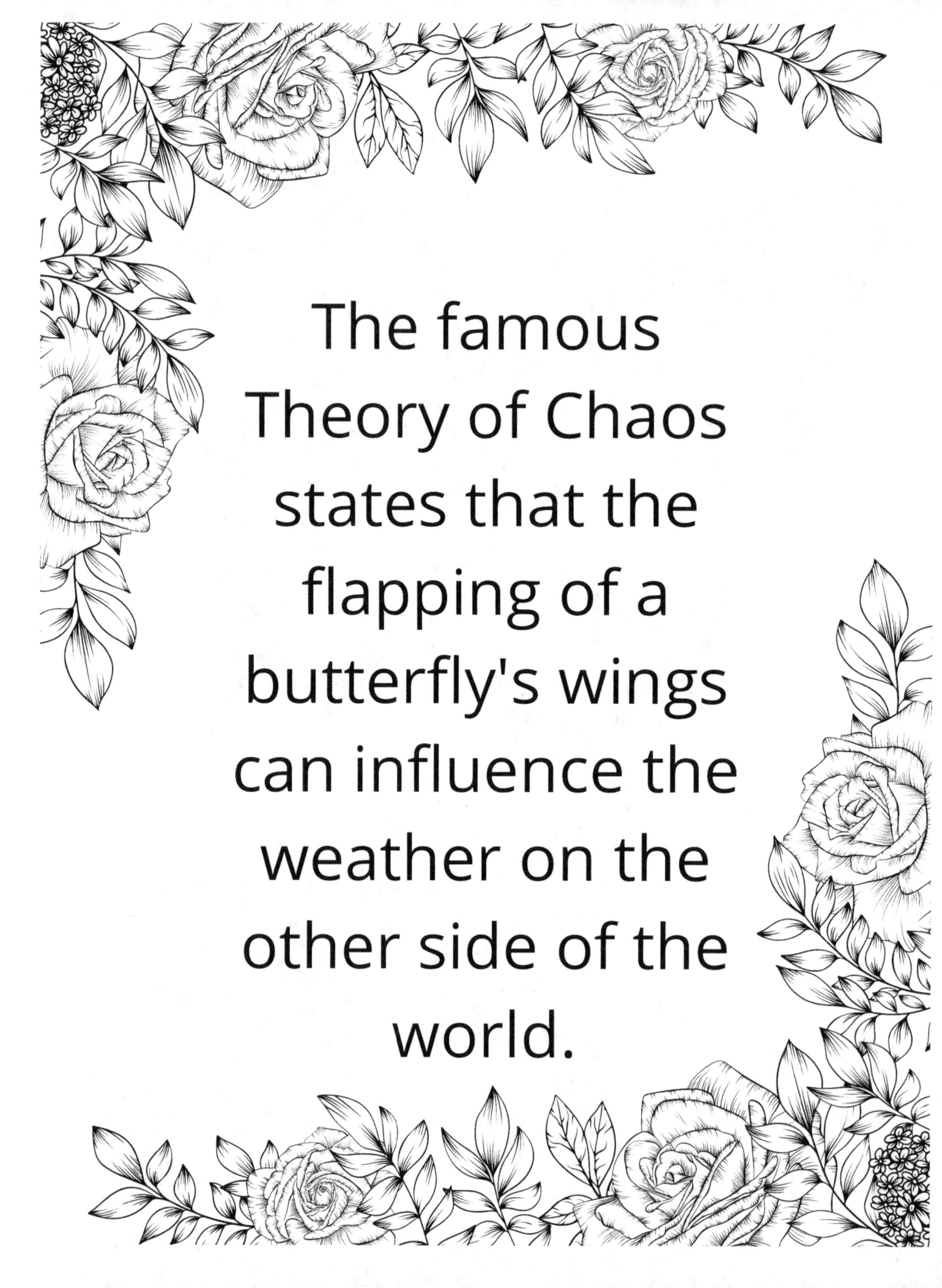

The famous Theory of Chaos states that the flapping of a butterfly's wings can influence the weather on the other side of the world.

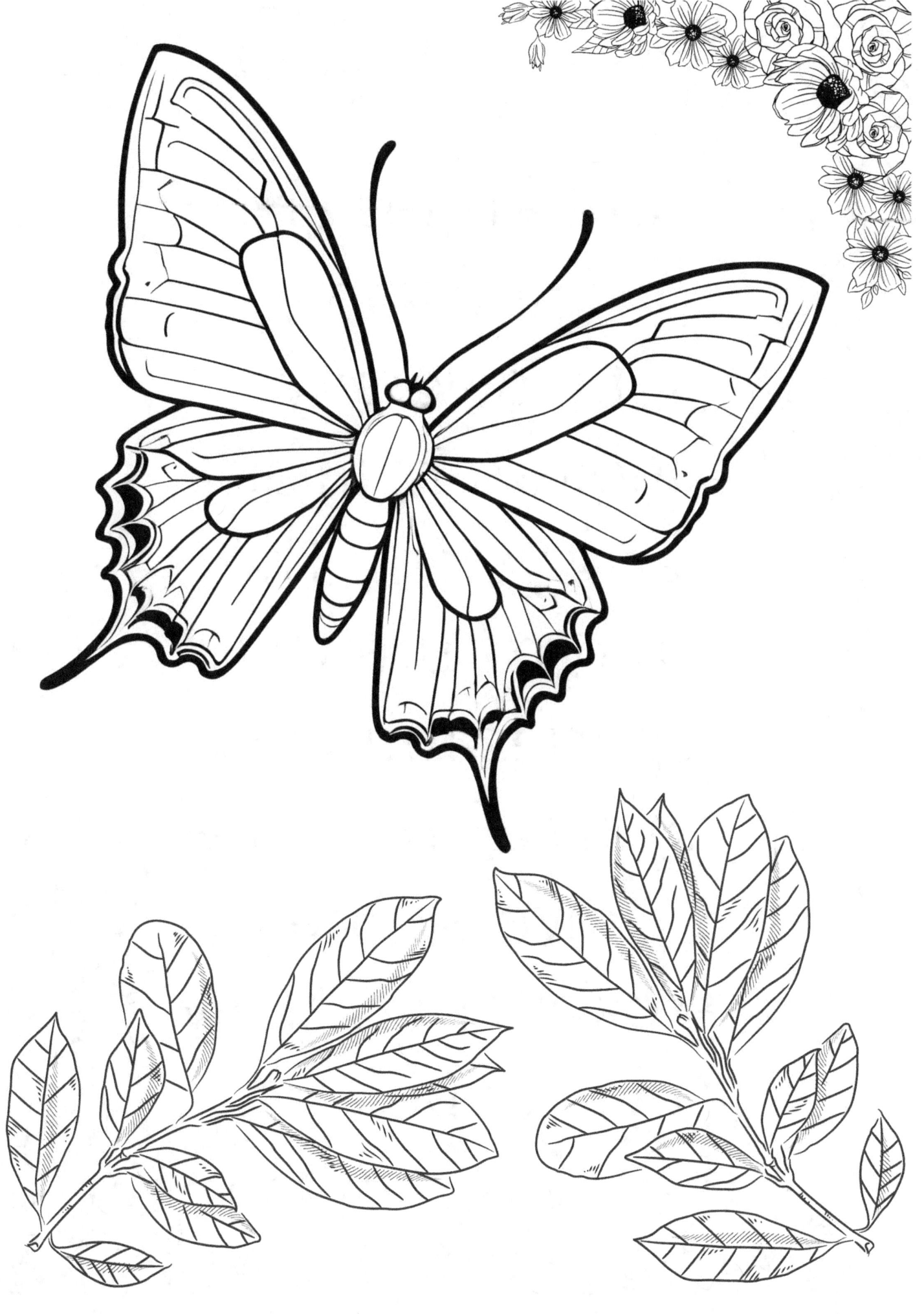

Butterflies are important biodiversity indicators in an ecosystem. The more butterfly species found in an area, the more diverse the ecosystem is likely to be.

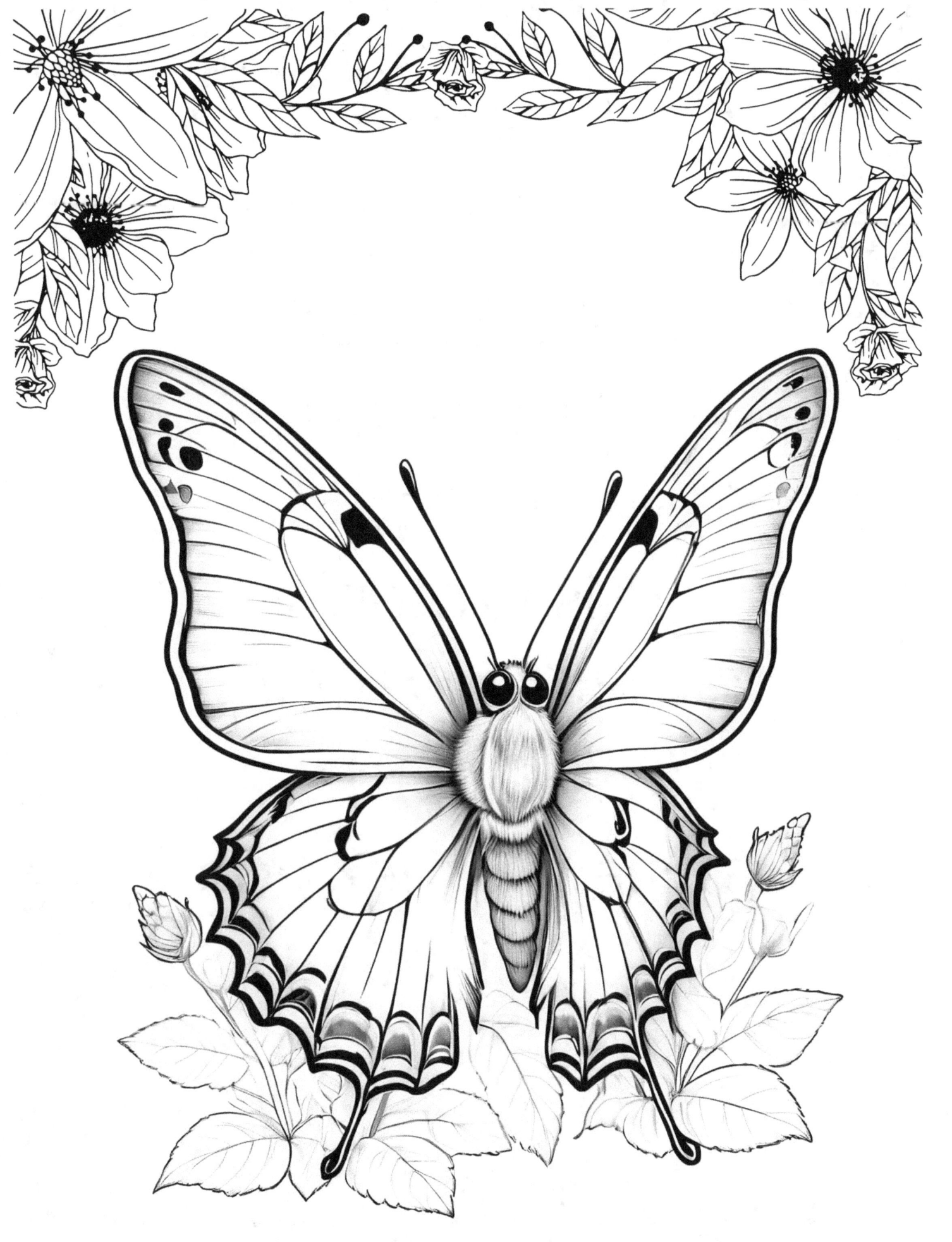

Apollo Butterfly (Parnassius apollo)
This butterfly owes its name to Apollo, the ancient Greek god of light.

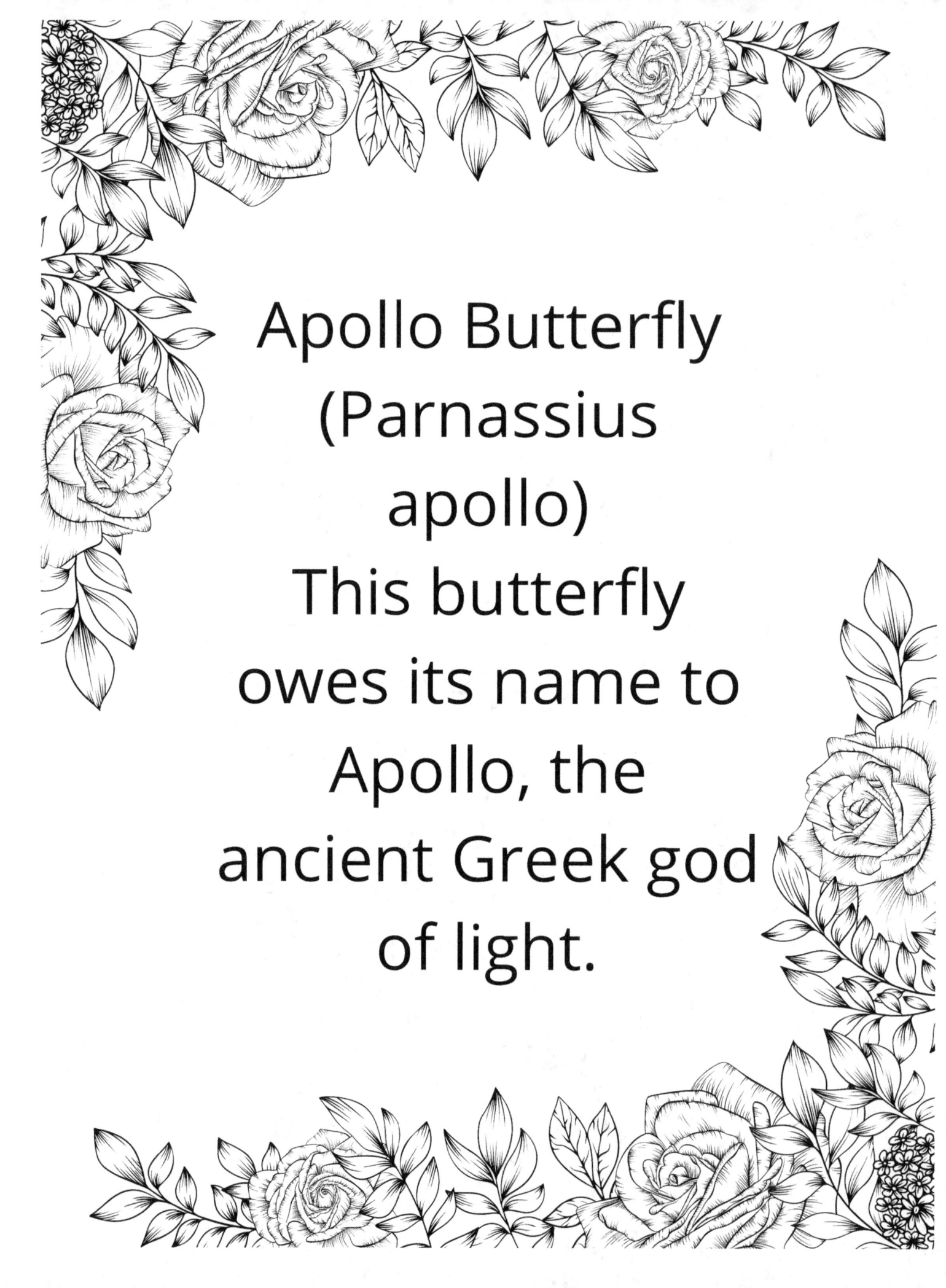

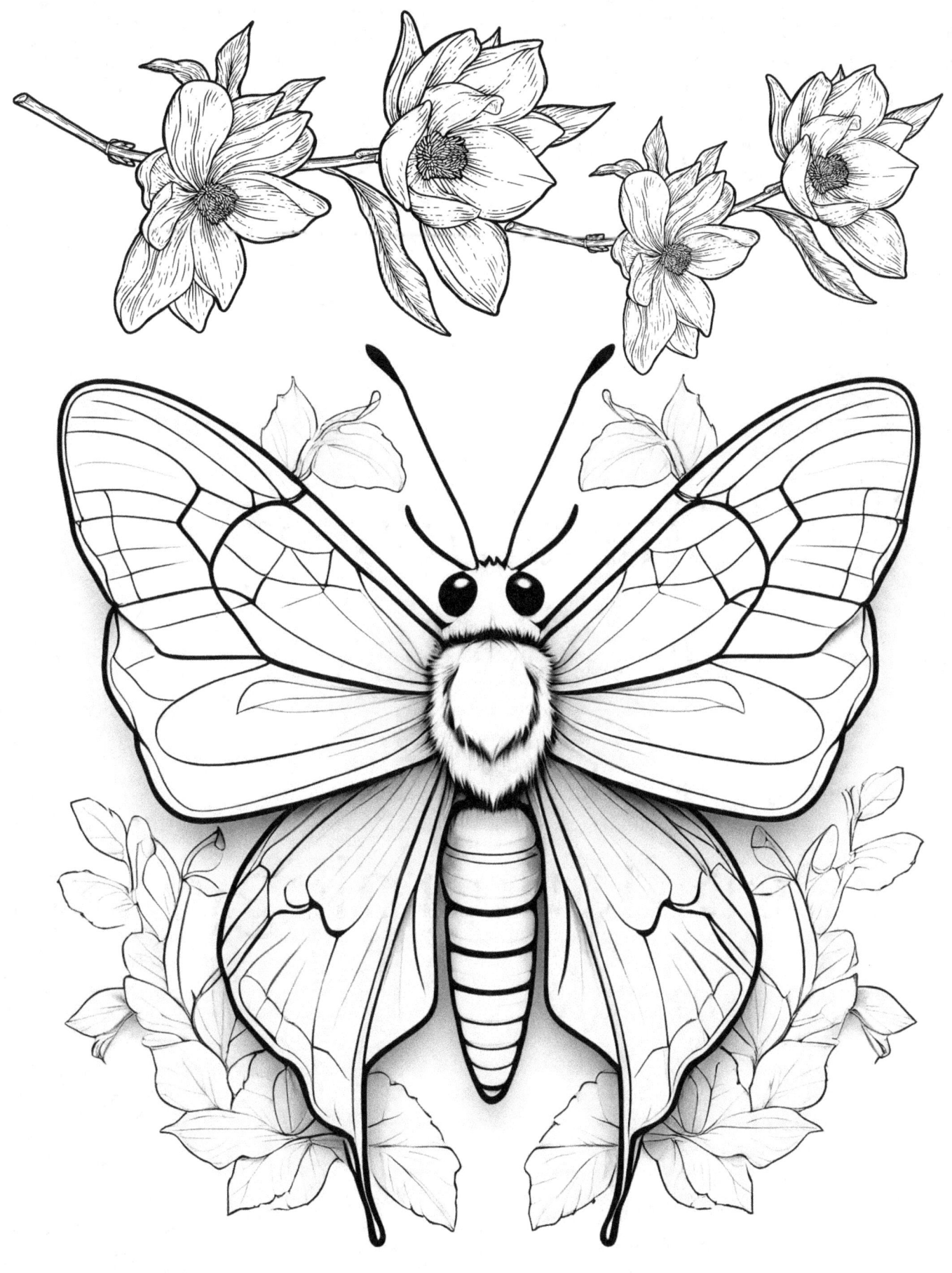

The study of butterflies is called lepidopterology.

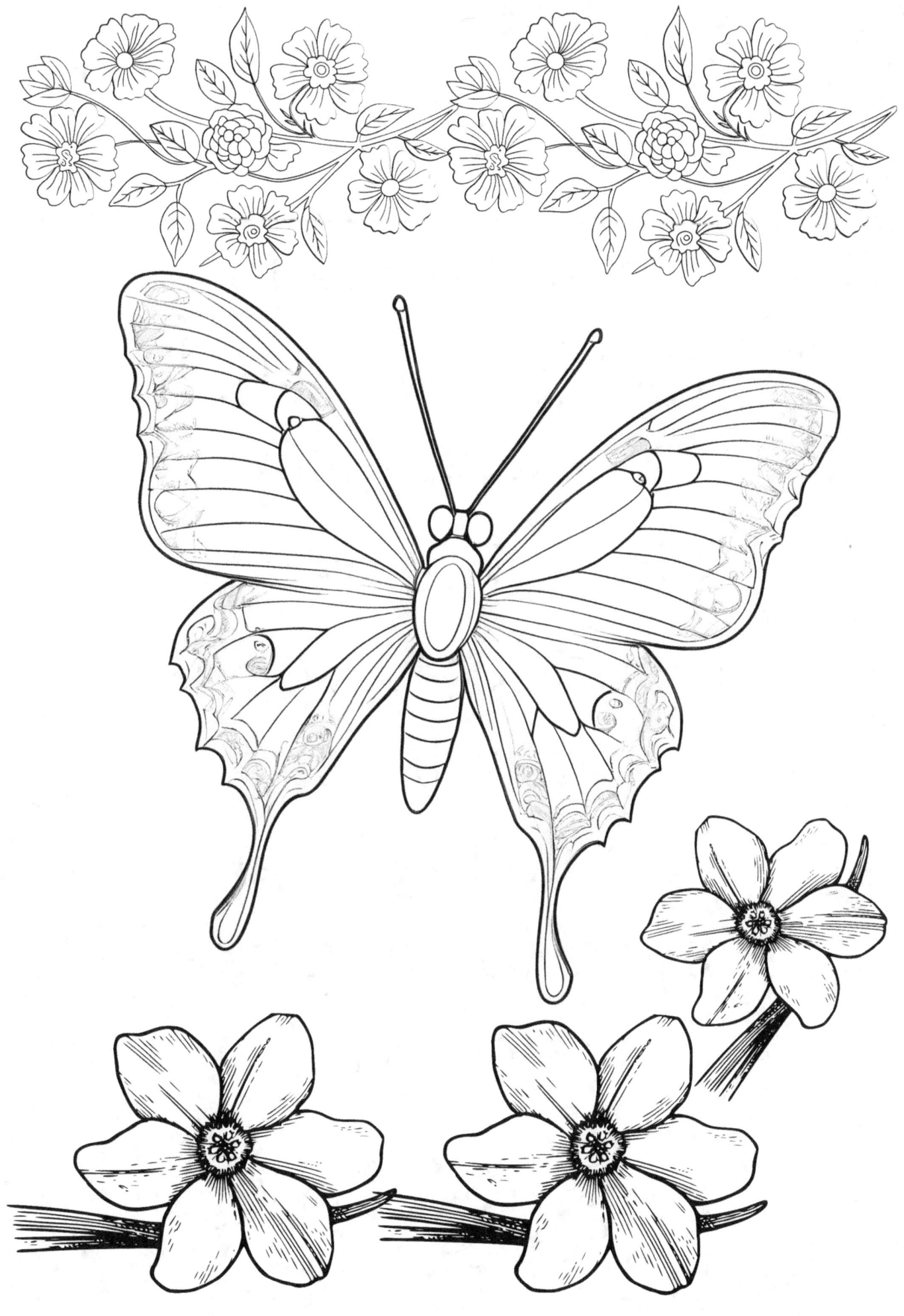

Owl Butterfly
(Caligo eurilochus brasiliensis)

When threatened, it suddenly opens its wings, revealing huge eyes, looking like an owl.

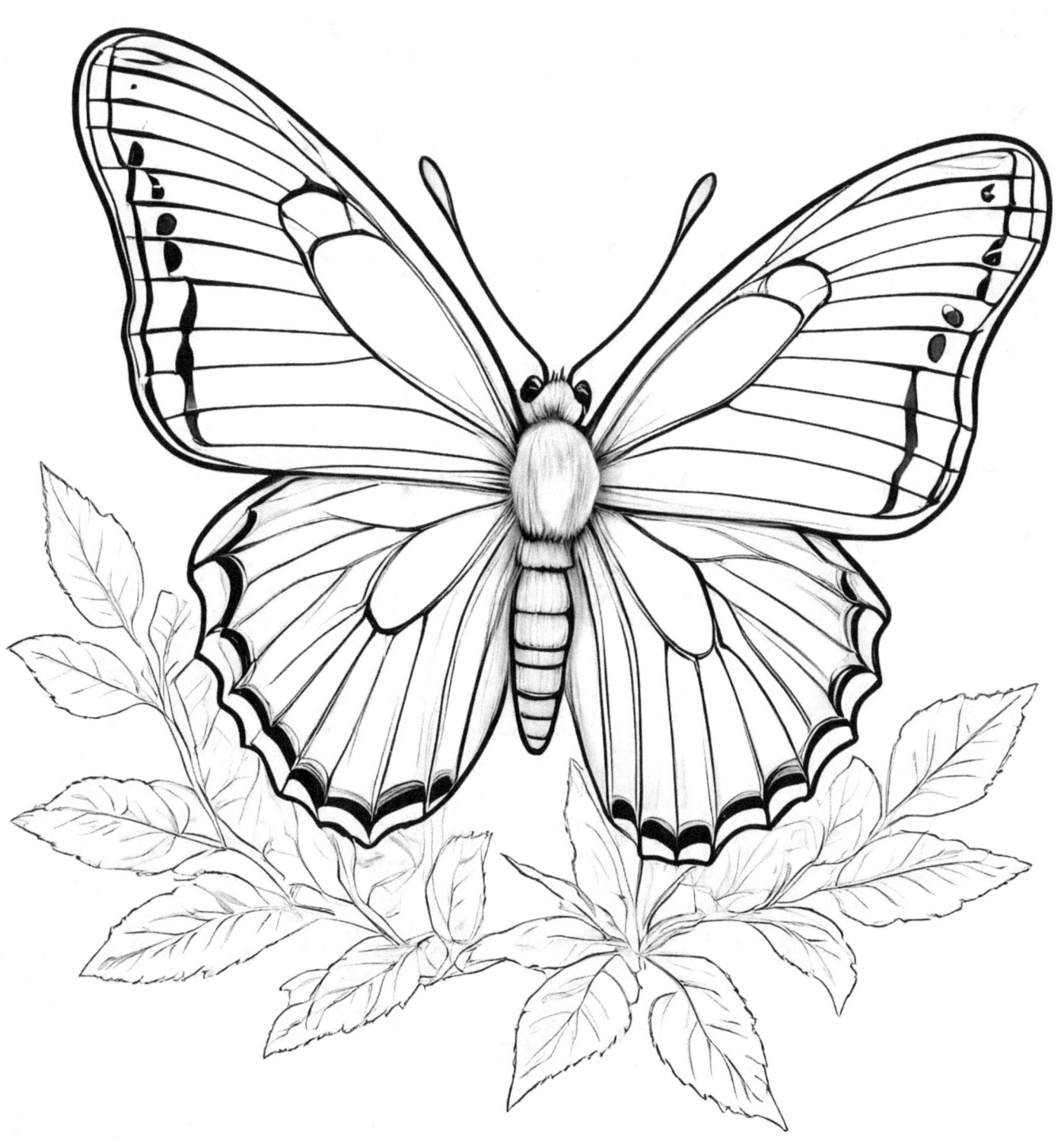

Some butterfly species, such as the Monarch Butterfly, undertake impressive annual migrations, traveling thousands of kilometers.

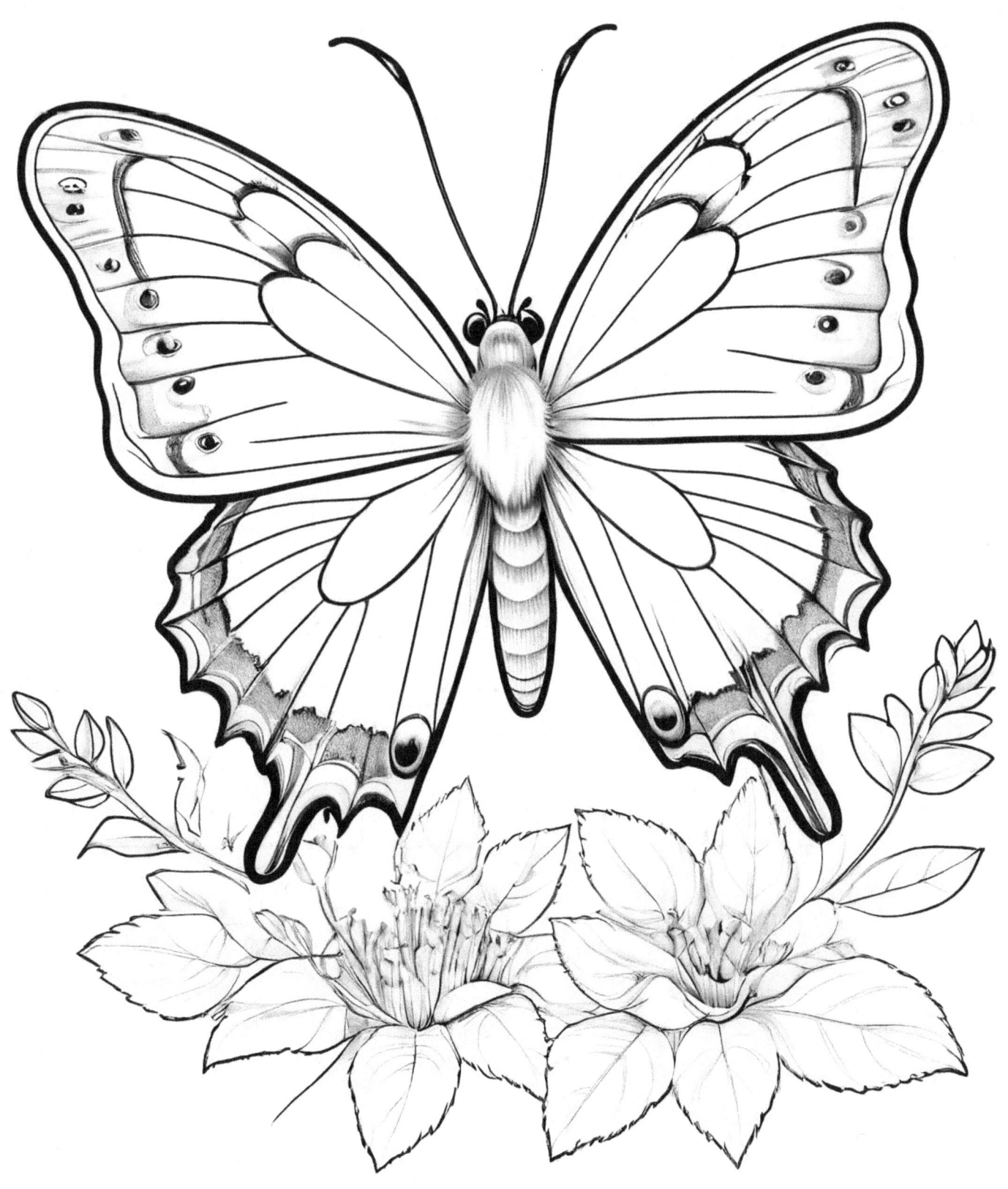

Flambeau Butterfly (Dryas Julia)
It is the species that has the longest lifespan, reaching up to six months of longevity.

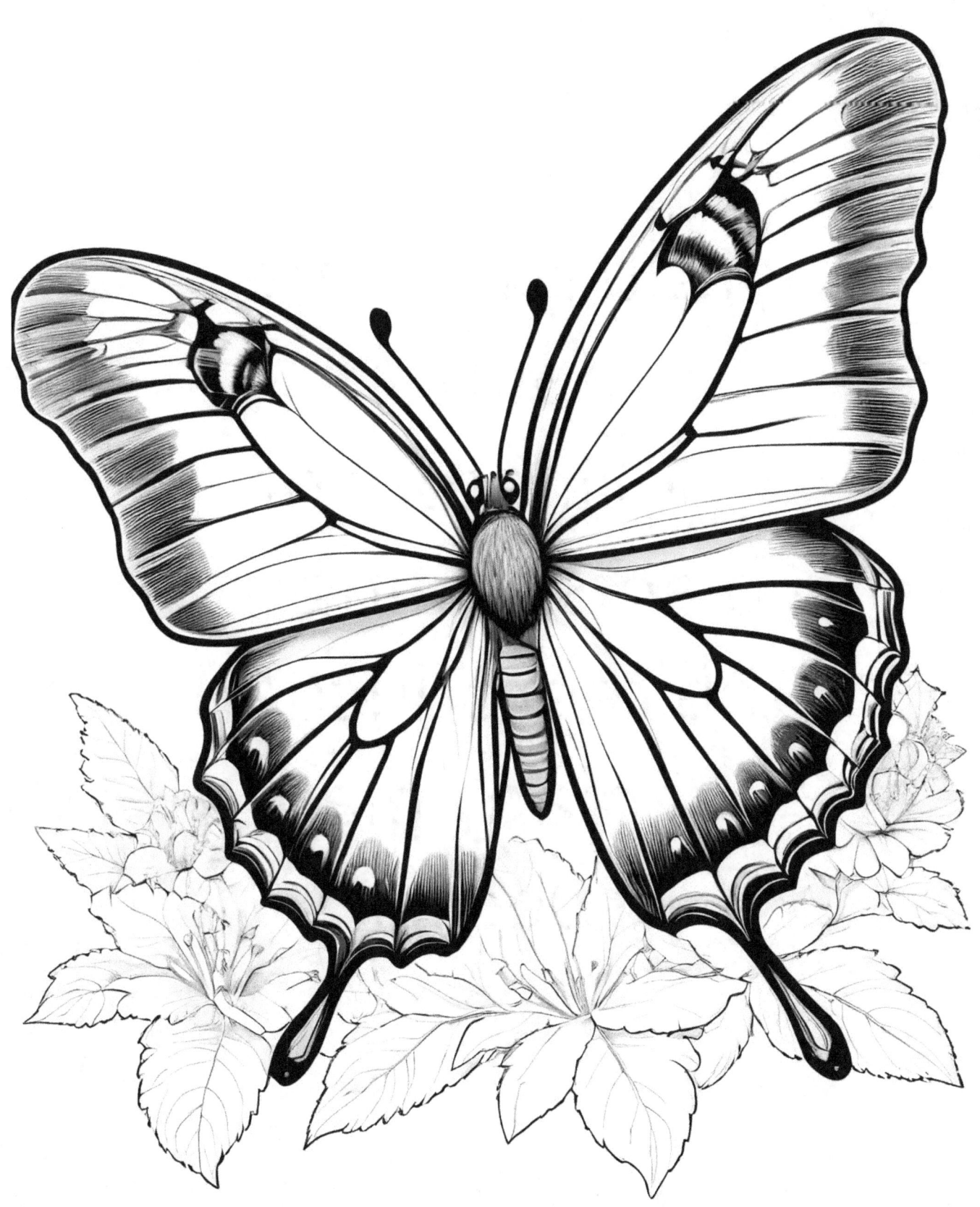

Butterflies are important pollinators of plants, aiding in the reproduction of many plant species.

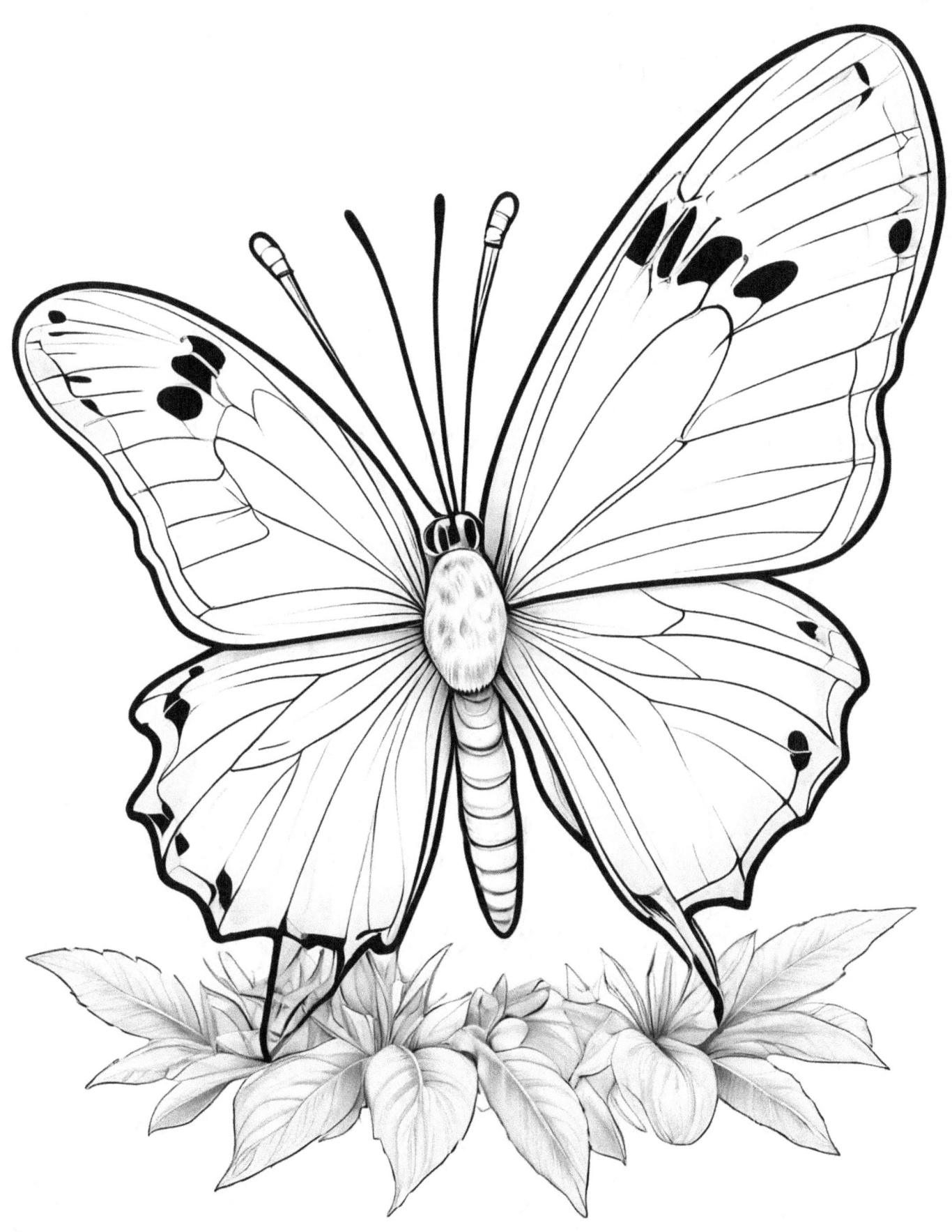

Swallowtail Butterfly
(Papilio machaon)
This butterfly lives in Europe, Asia and cold regions of North America.

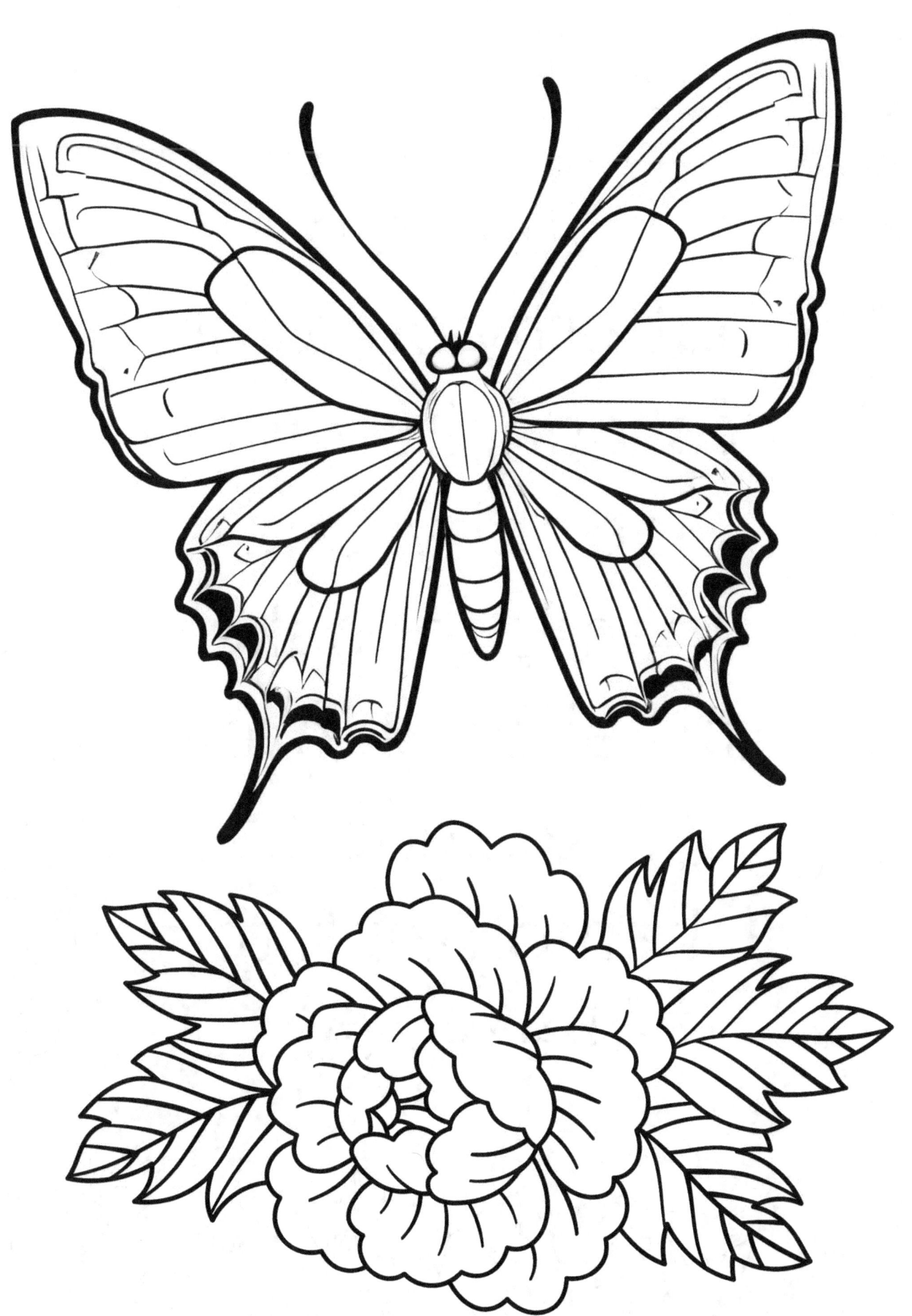

If you help a butterfly out of its cocoon, its wings atrophy. She needs to make this effort in order to send hemolymph to the wings.

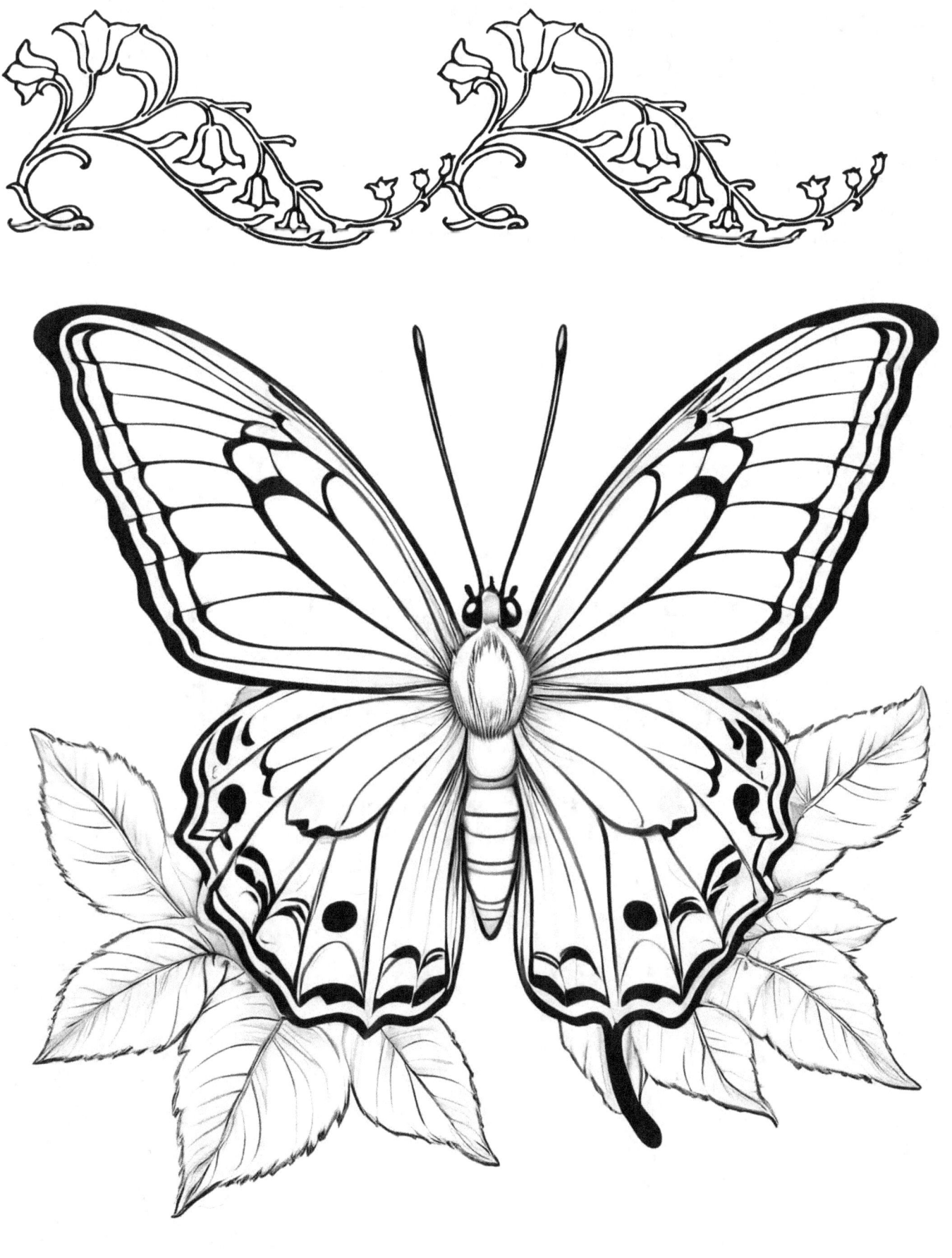

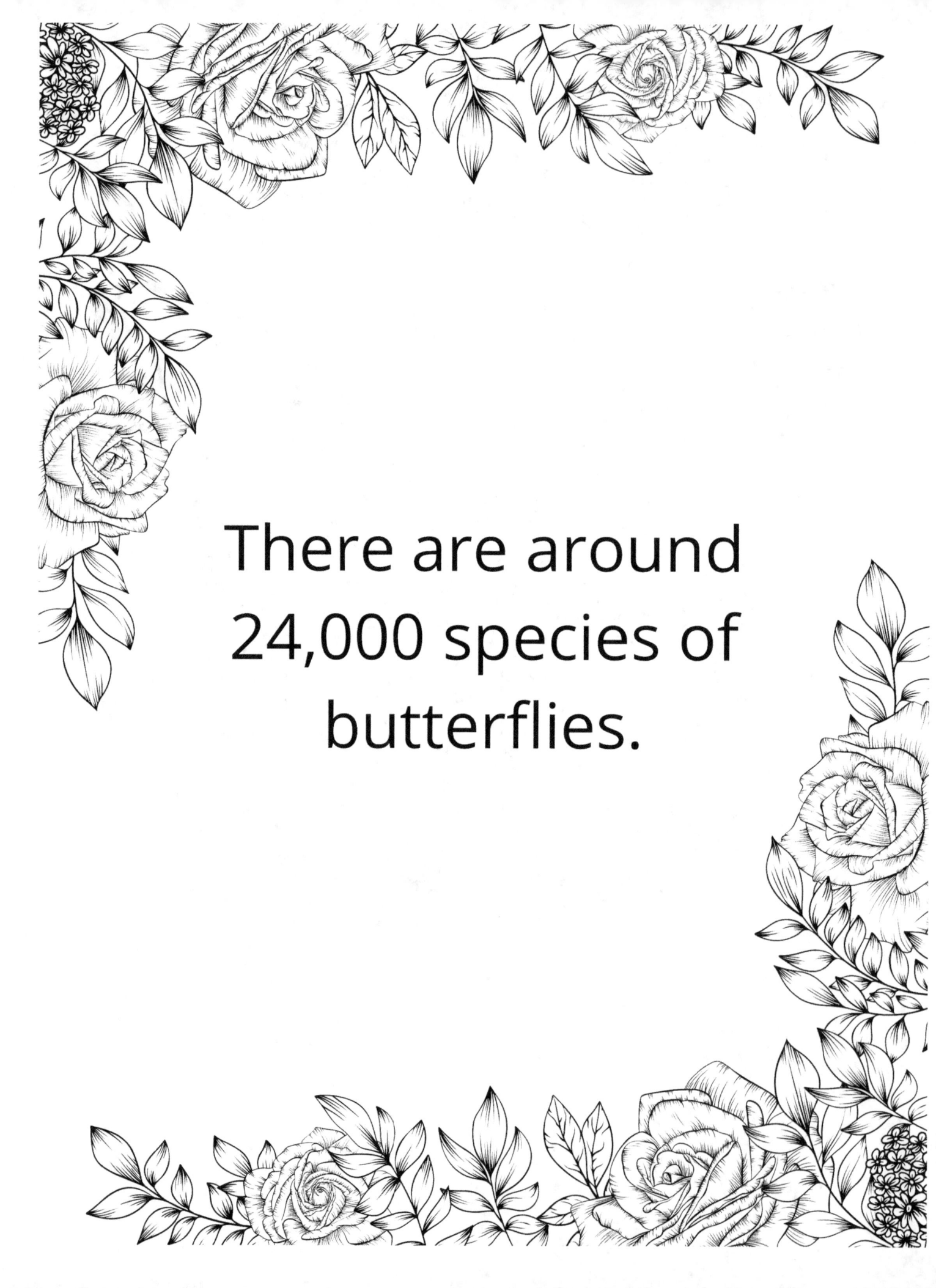

There are around 24,000 species of butterflies.

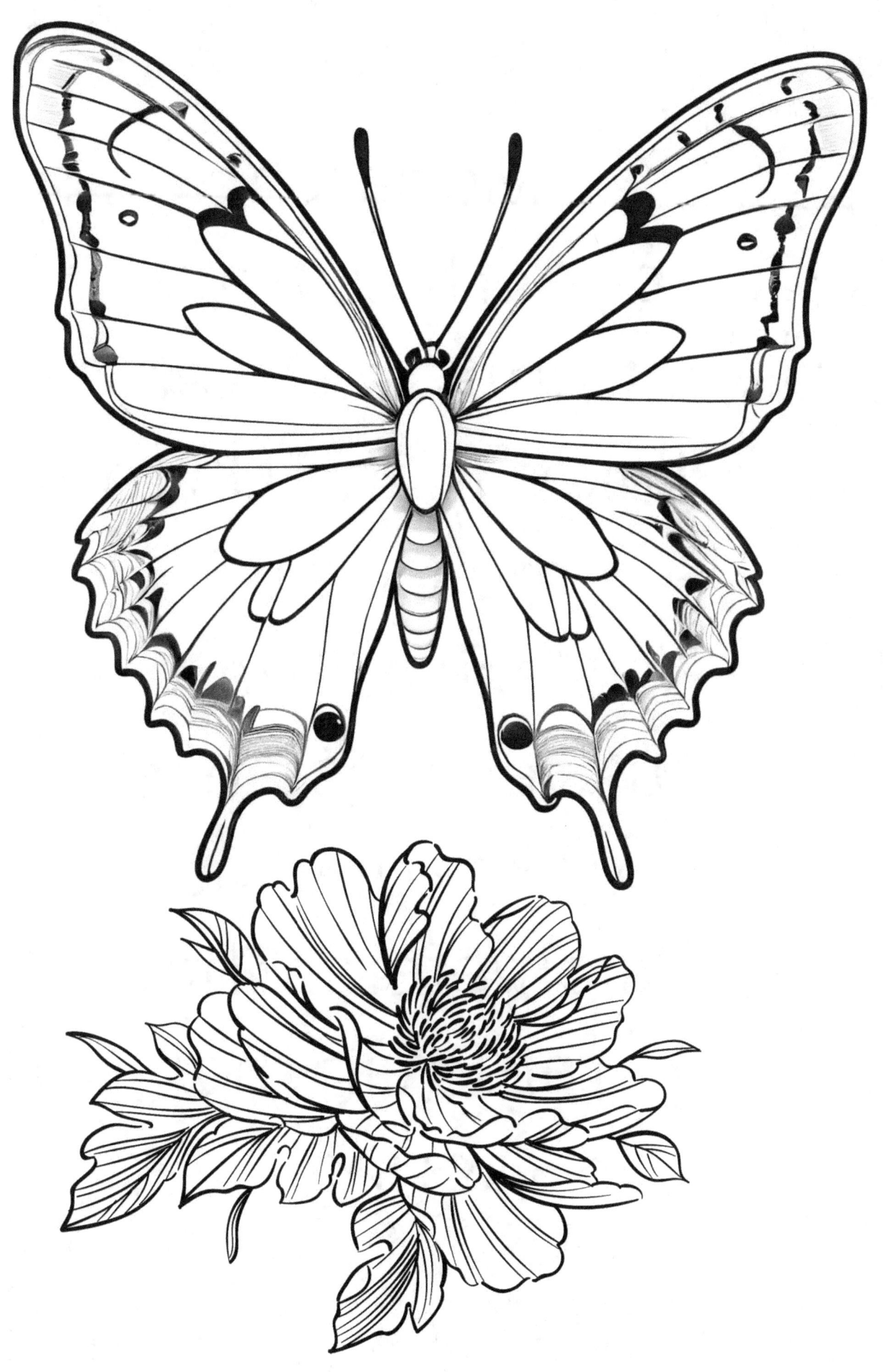

Monarch butterflies travel from the Great Lakes in the US to the Gulf of Mexico. They travel a distance of 3 thousand kilometers. They return in the spring.

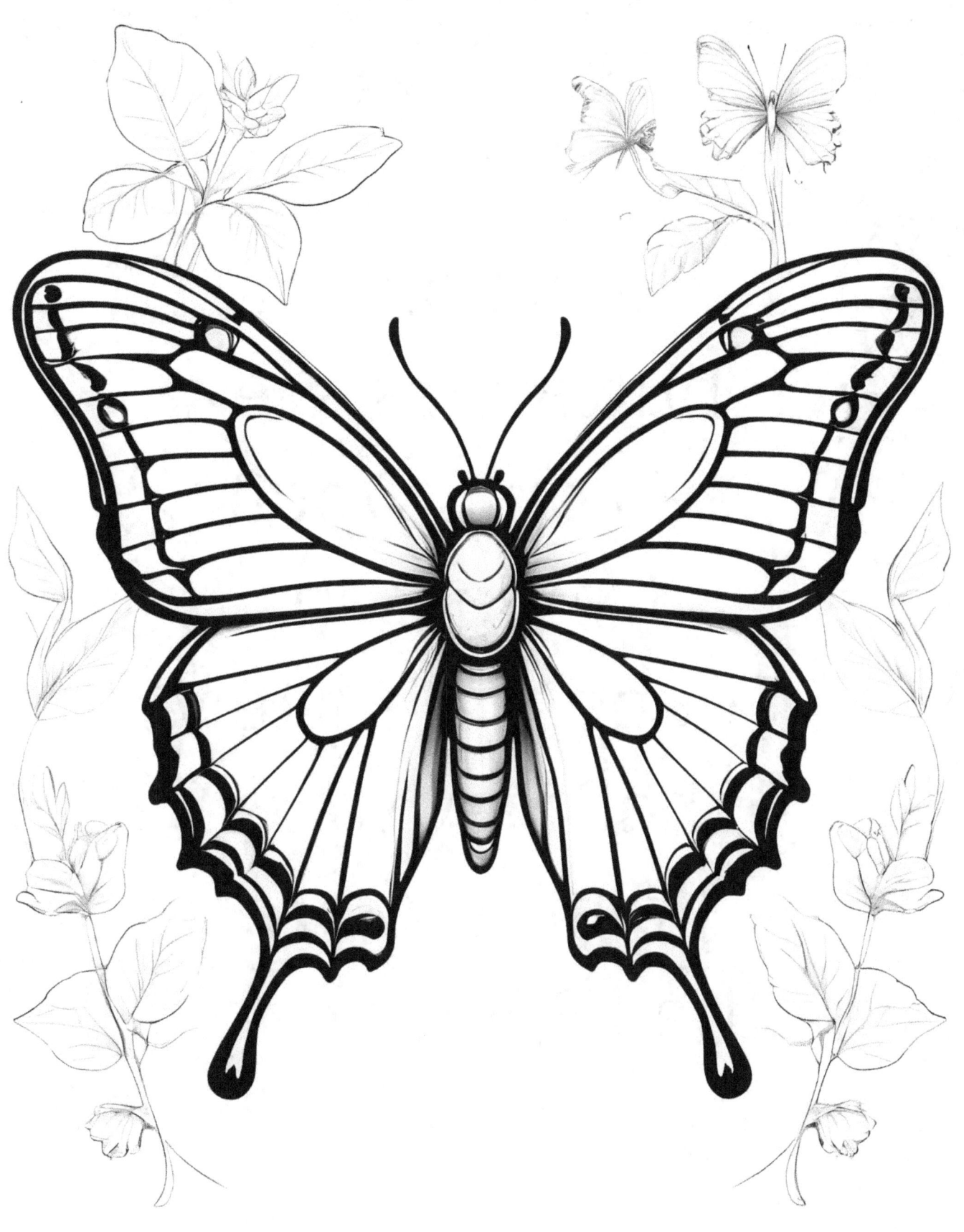

Depictions of butterflies are seen on Egyptian frescoes in Thebes. It is likely that they were painted more than 3,500 years ago.

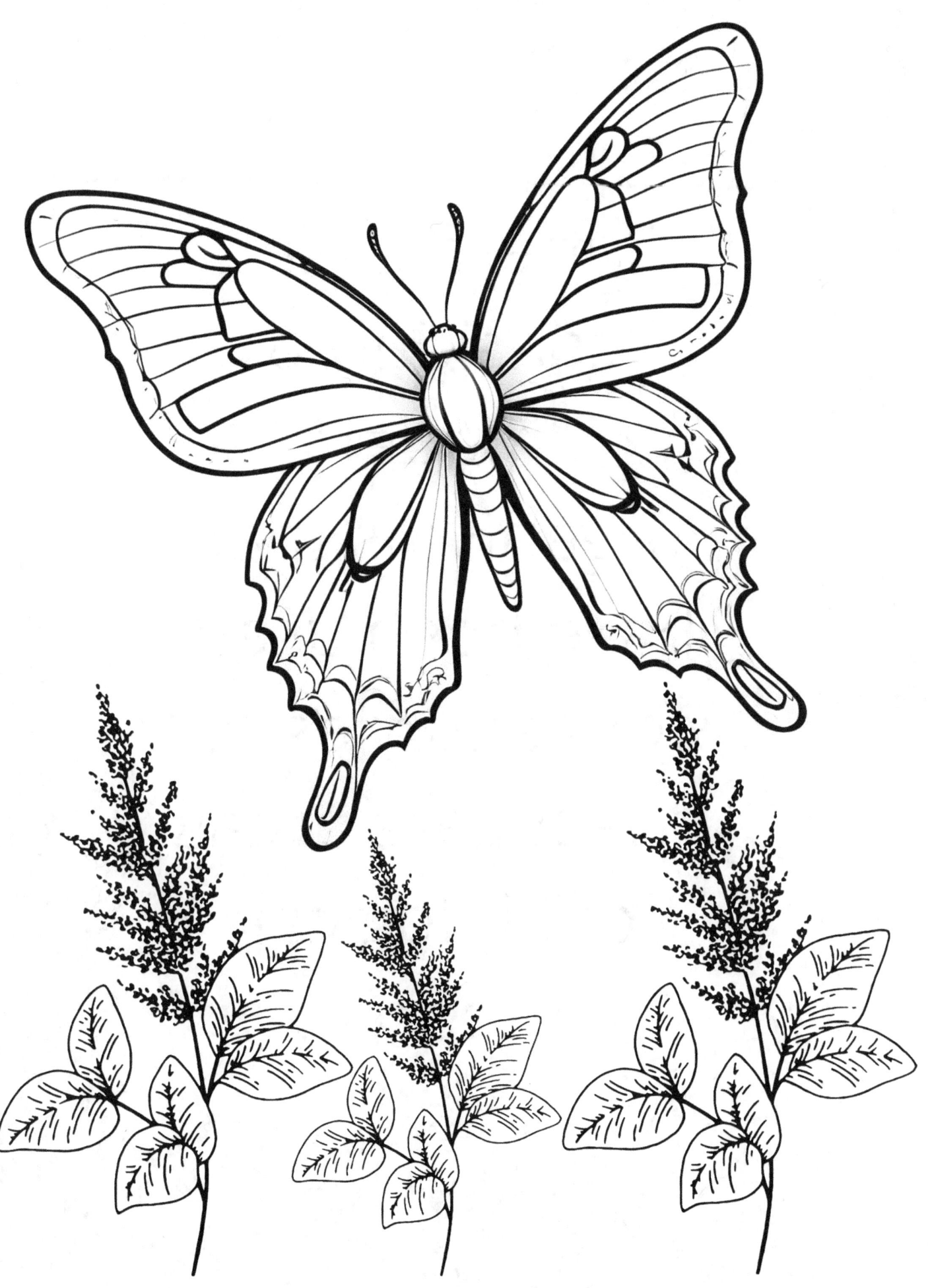

Butterflies are considered "model" organisms that have been used for centuries to investigate areas of biological research.

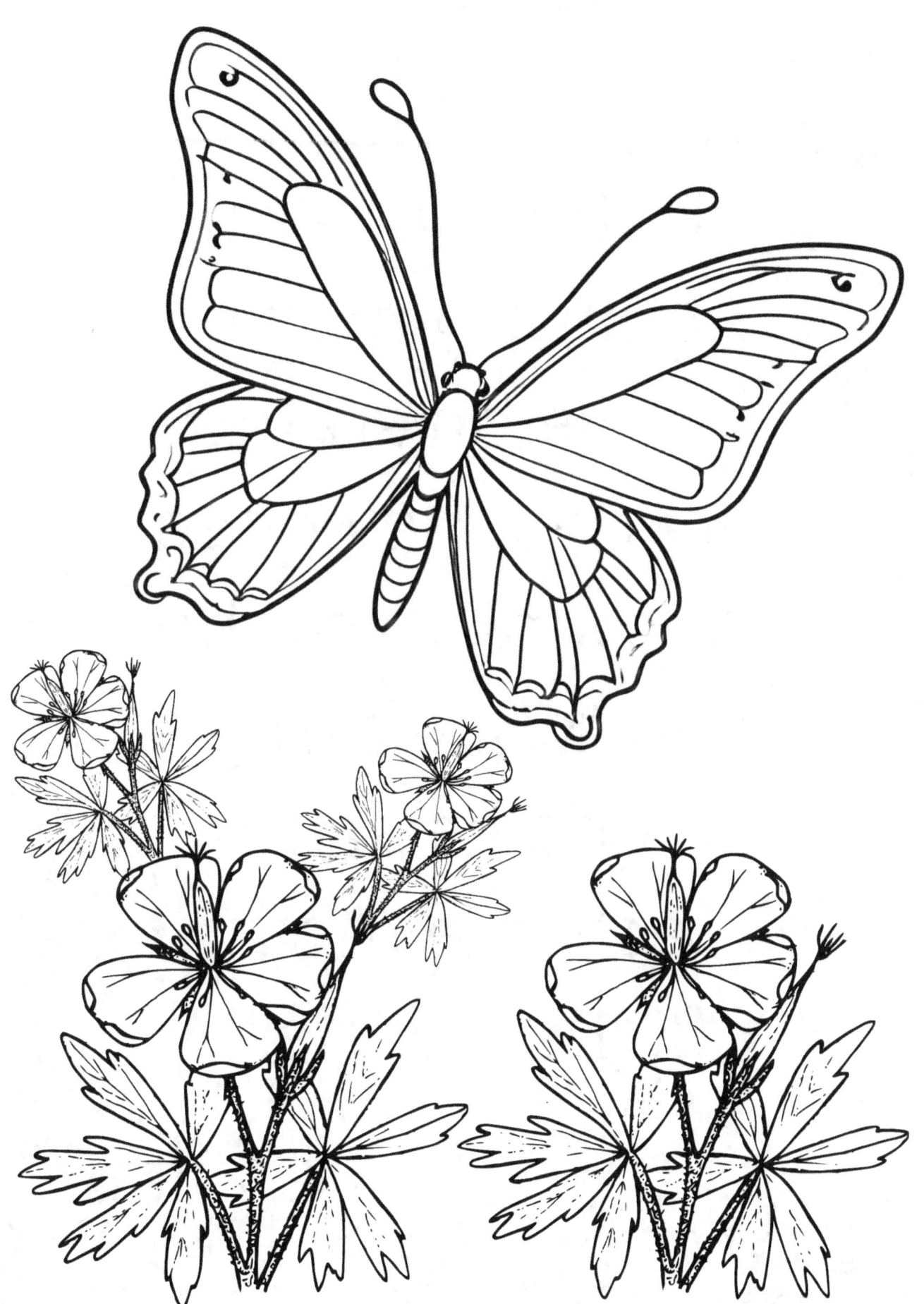

Butterflies are typically more active on sunny days, as they need the warmth of the sun to heat their bodies and activate their flight muscles.

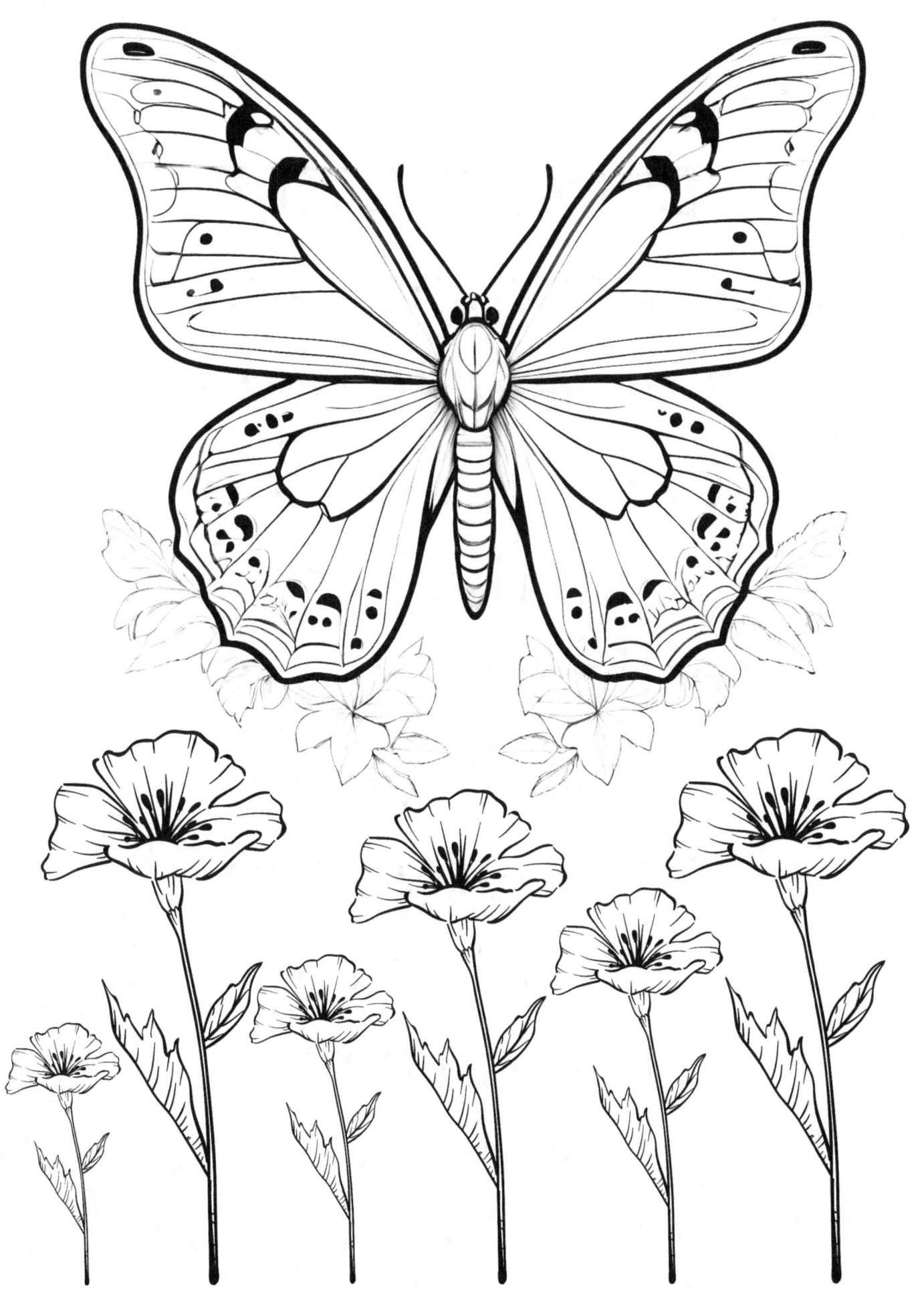

Butterflies can experiment with their feet, in order to find out if the leaf they are resting on is good for laying eggs and being food for their caterpillars.

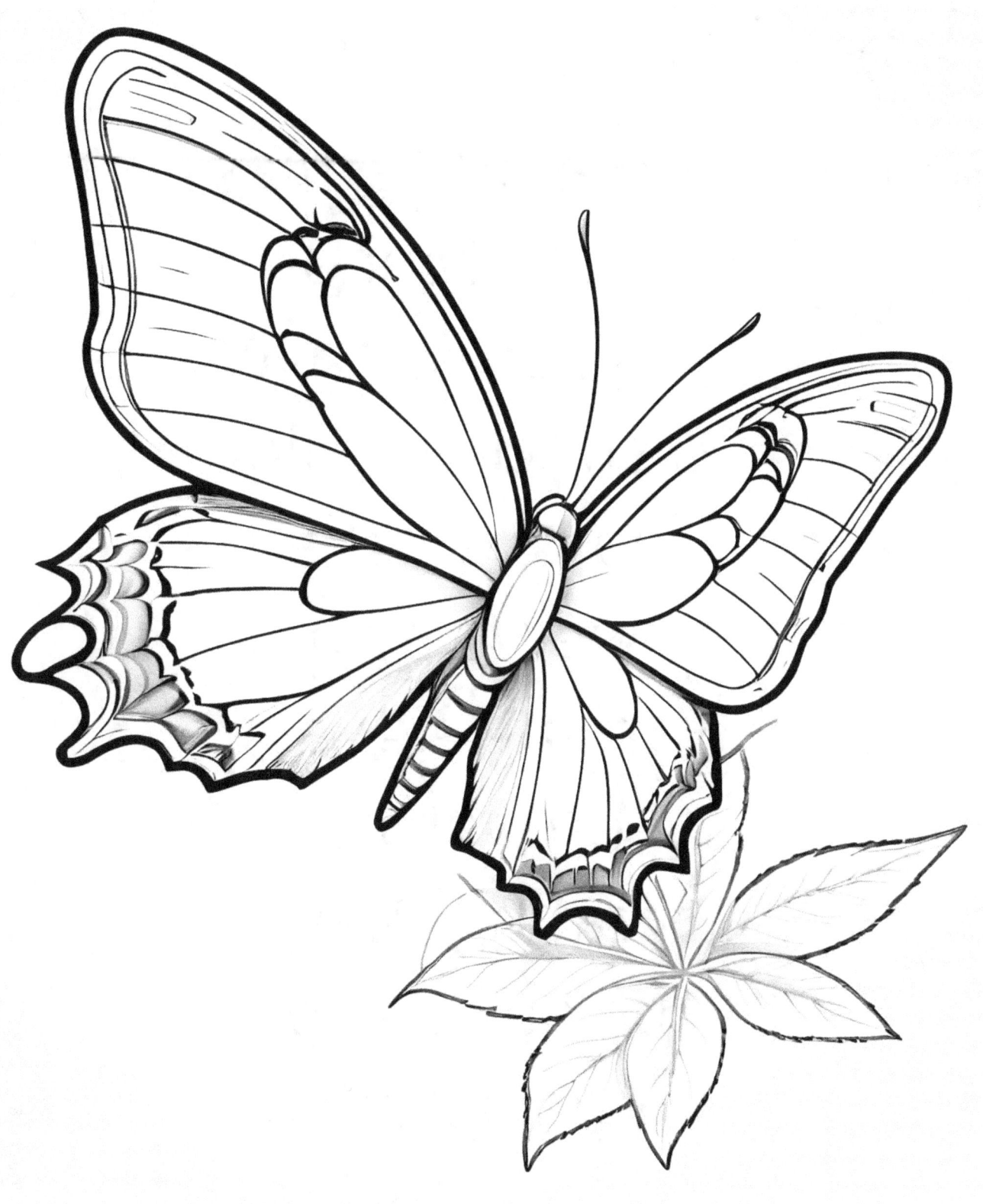

Some butterflies, like the Monarch butterfly, have distinctive color patterns that serve as a warning signal to predators, indicating they are poisonous or unpalatable to eat.

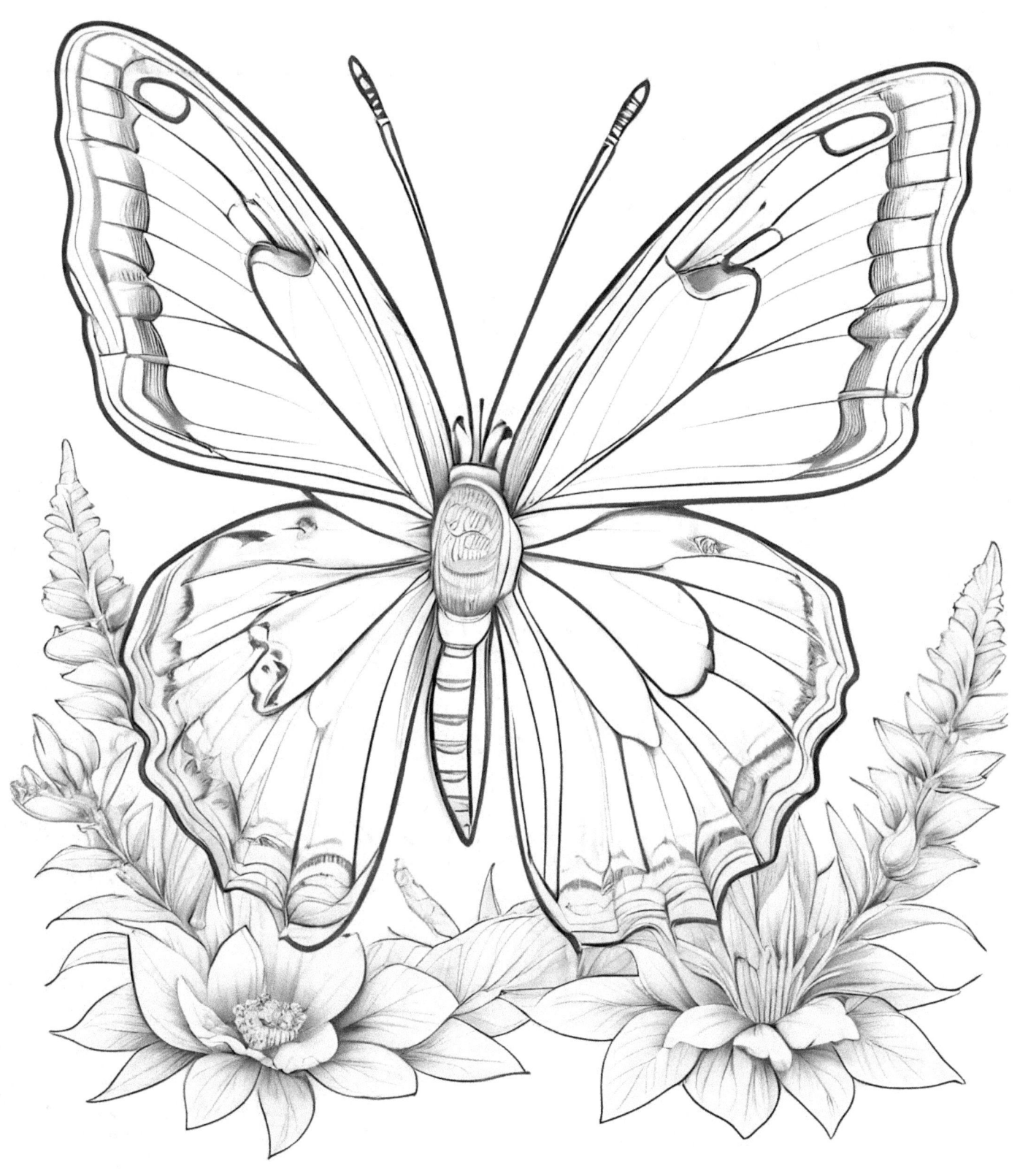

When the caterpillars complete their development, they stop feeding and look for a suitable place for the pupal stage.

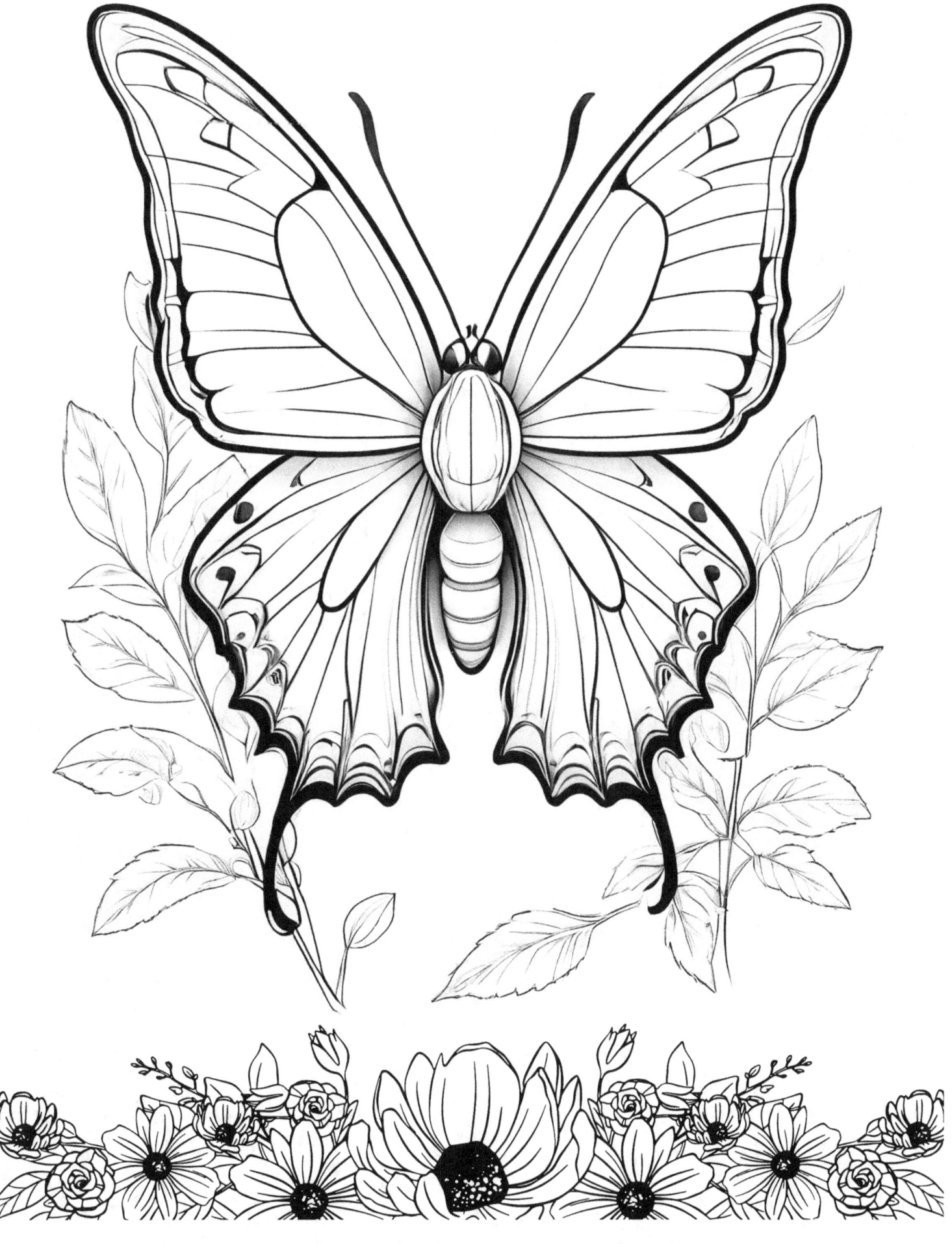

The scientific name of the Monarch is Danaus plexippus.

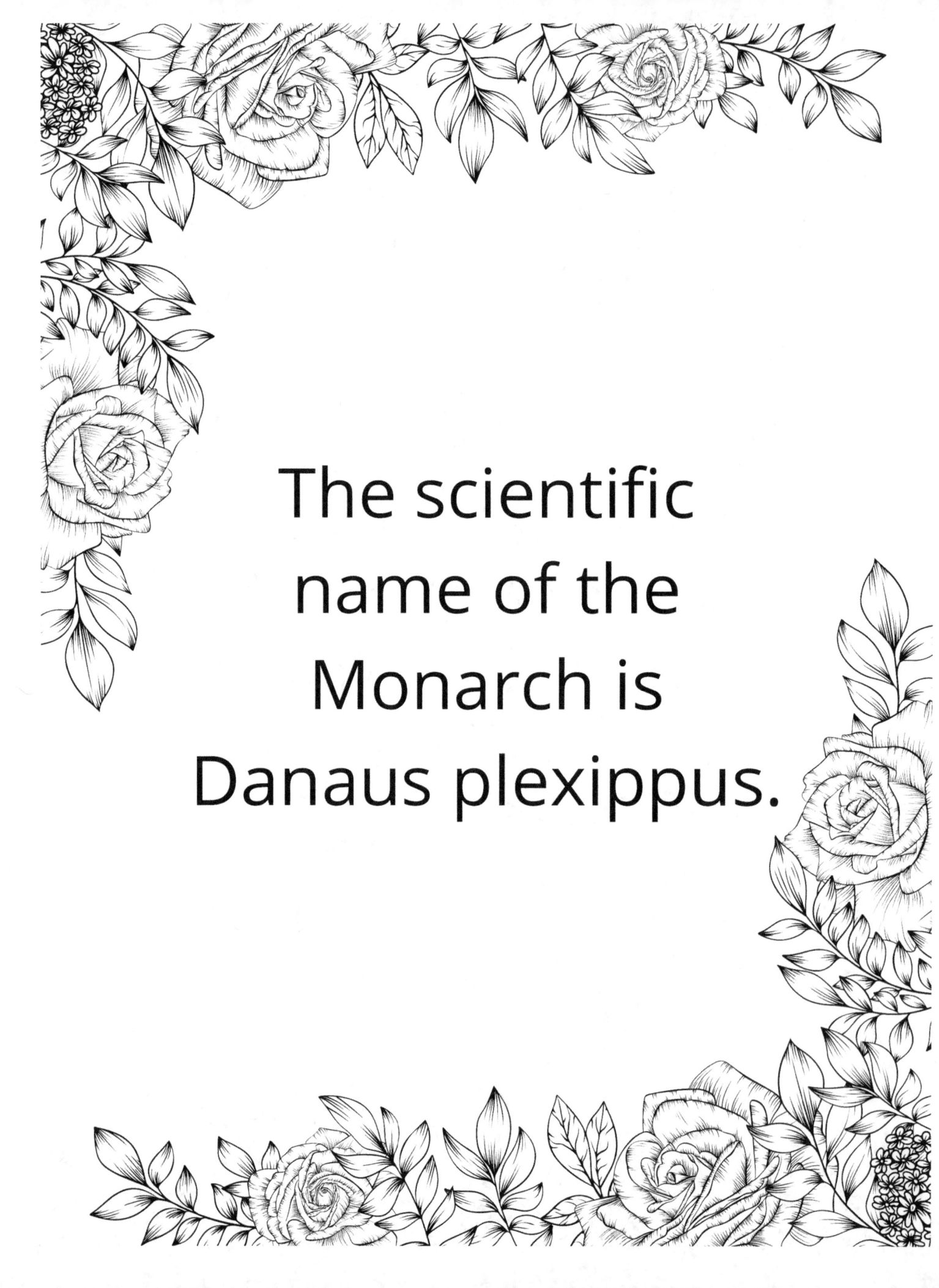

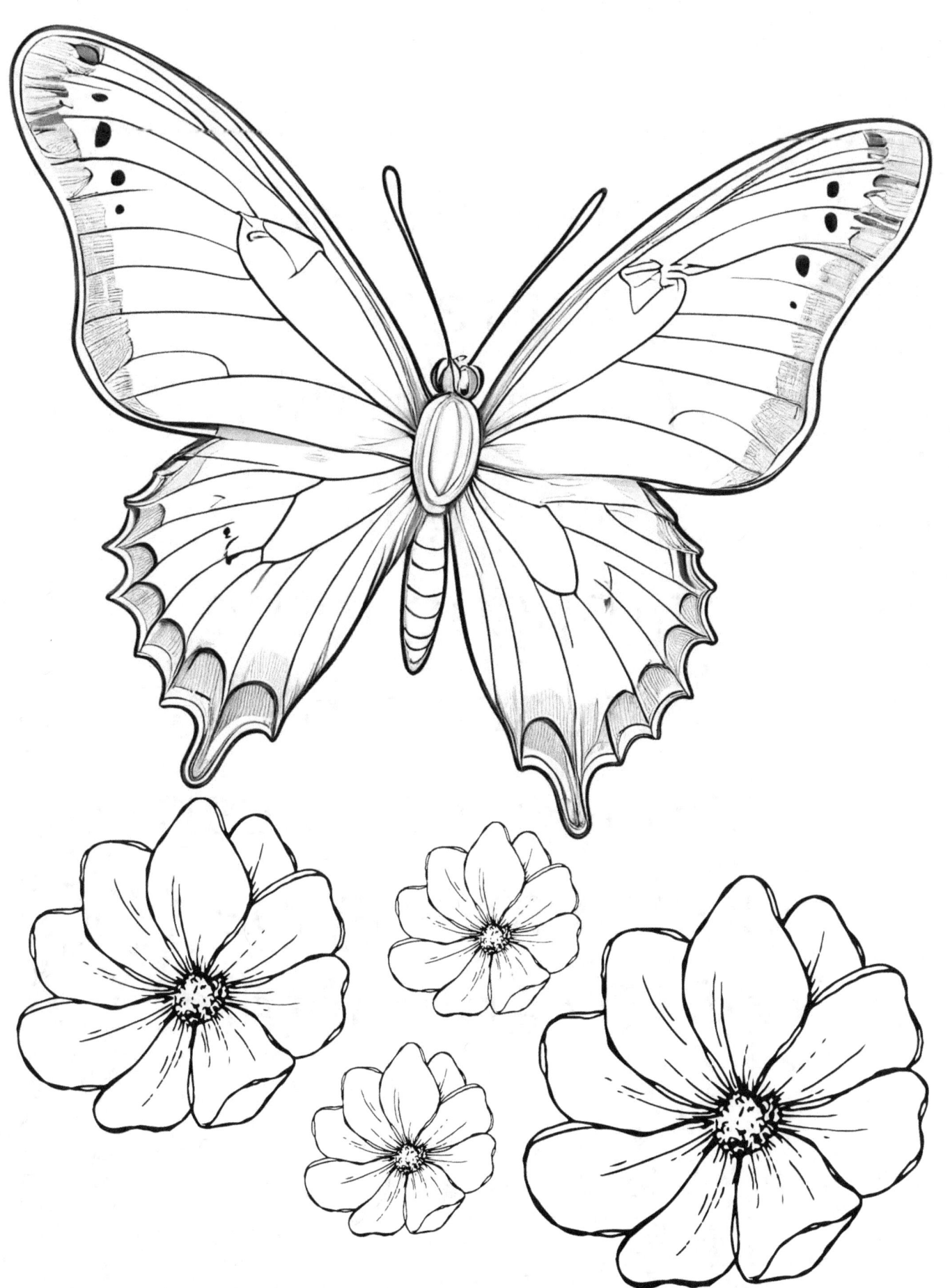

Swallowtail Butterfly.
This butterfly is still found throughout the American continent and can reach a wingspan of 10 centimeters.

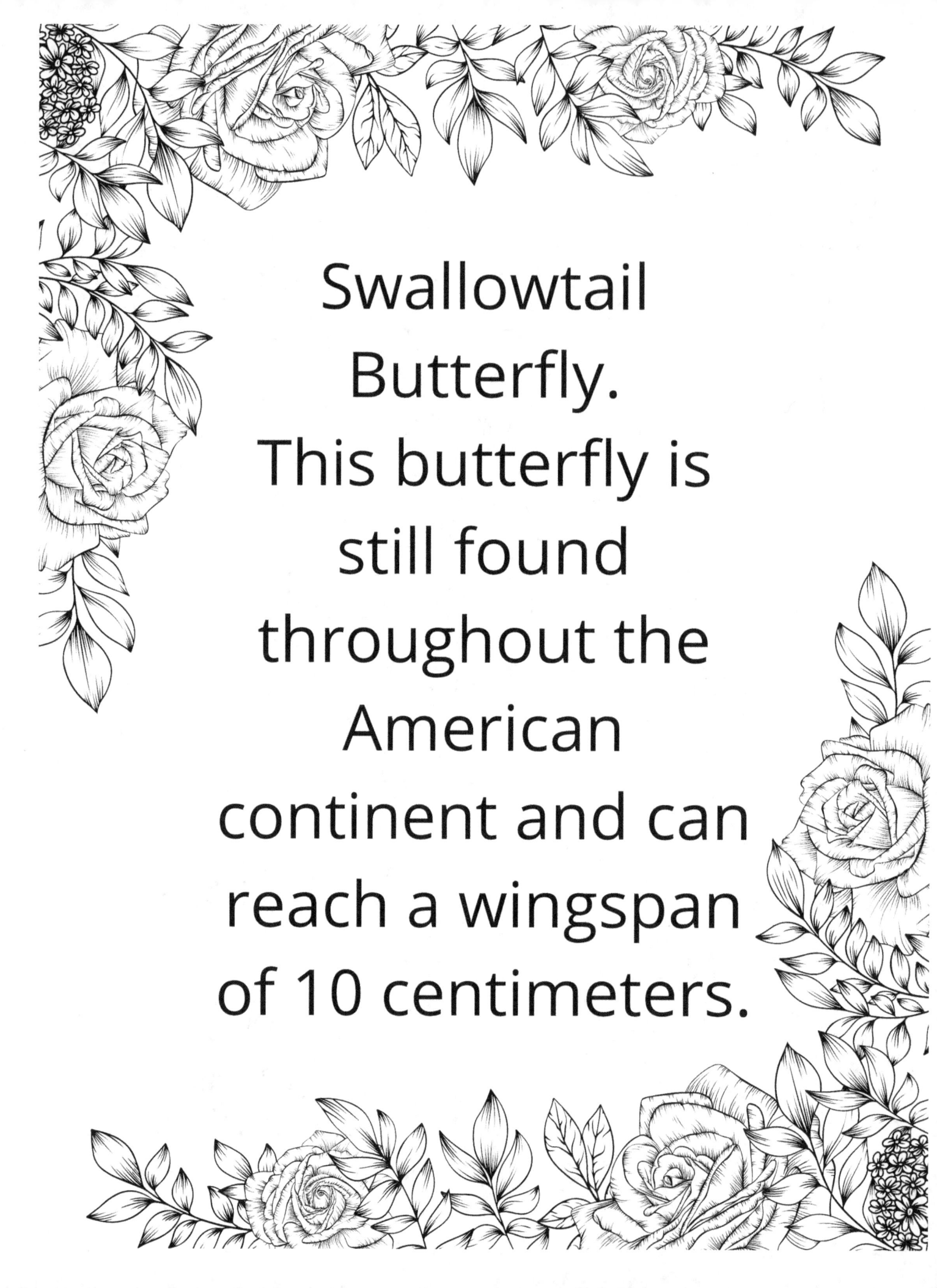

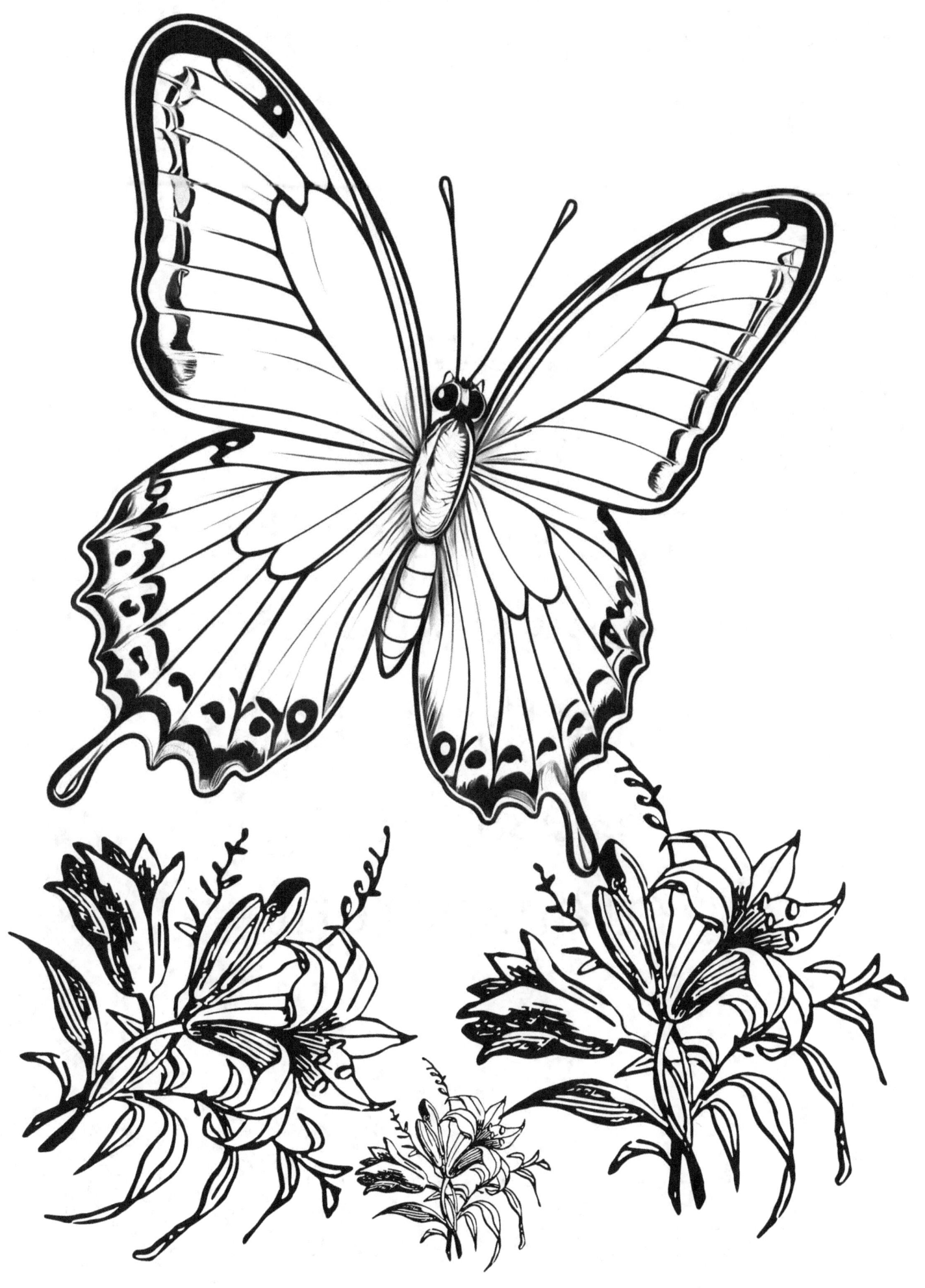

Glasswinged Butterfly.
The wing of the glasswinged butterfly looks like glass, being transparent.

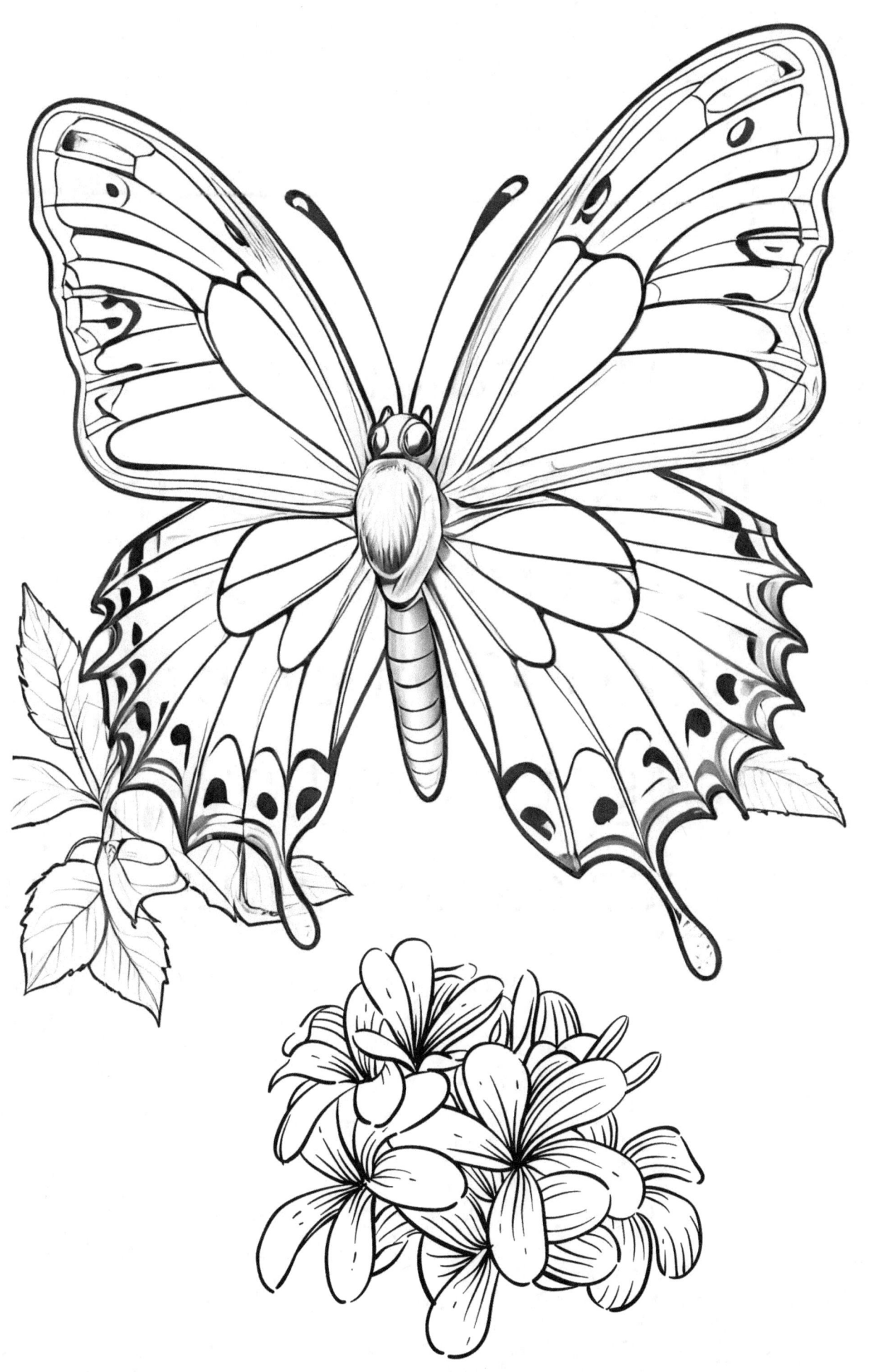

The color of a butterfly's wings is determined by the reflection of light from tiny scales covering them.

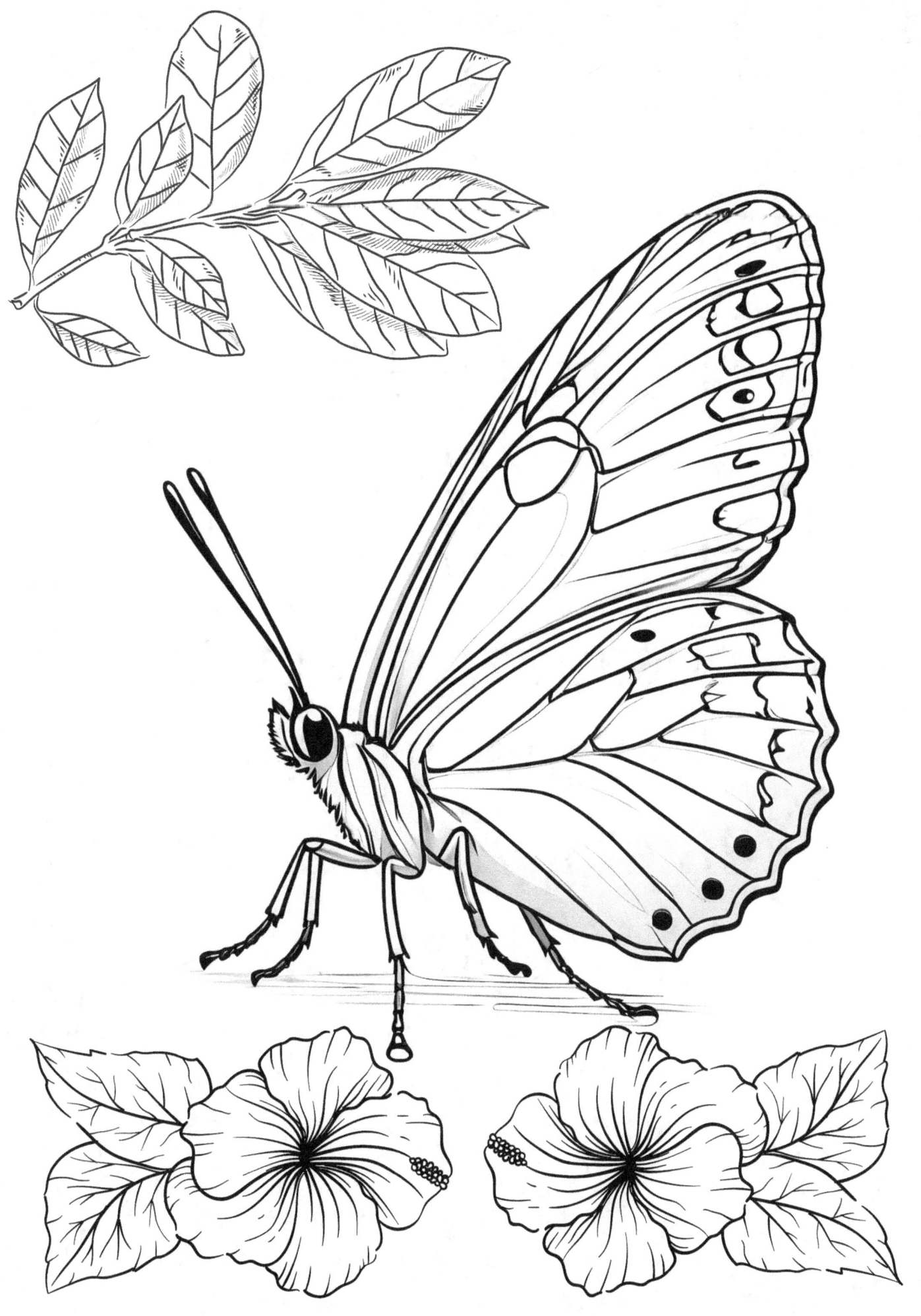

Butterfly Eighty-Eight.
It has this name because, in fact, it has the number 88 engraved on its wing.

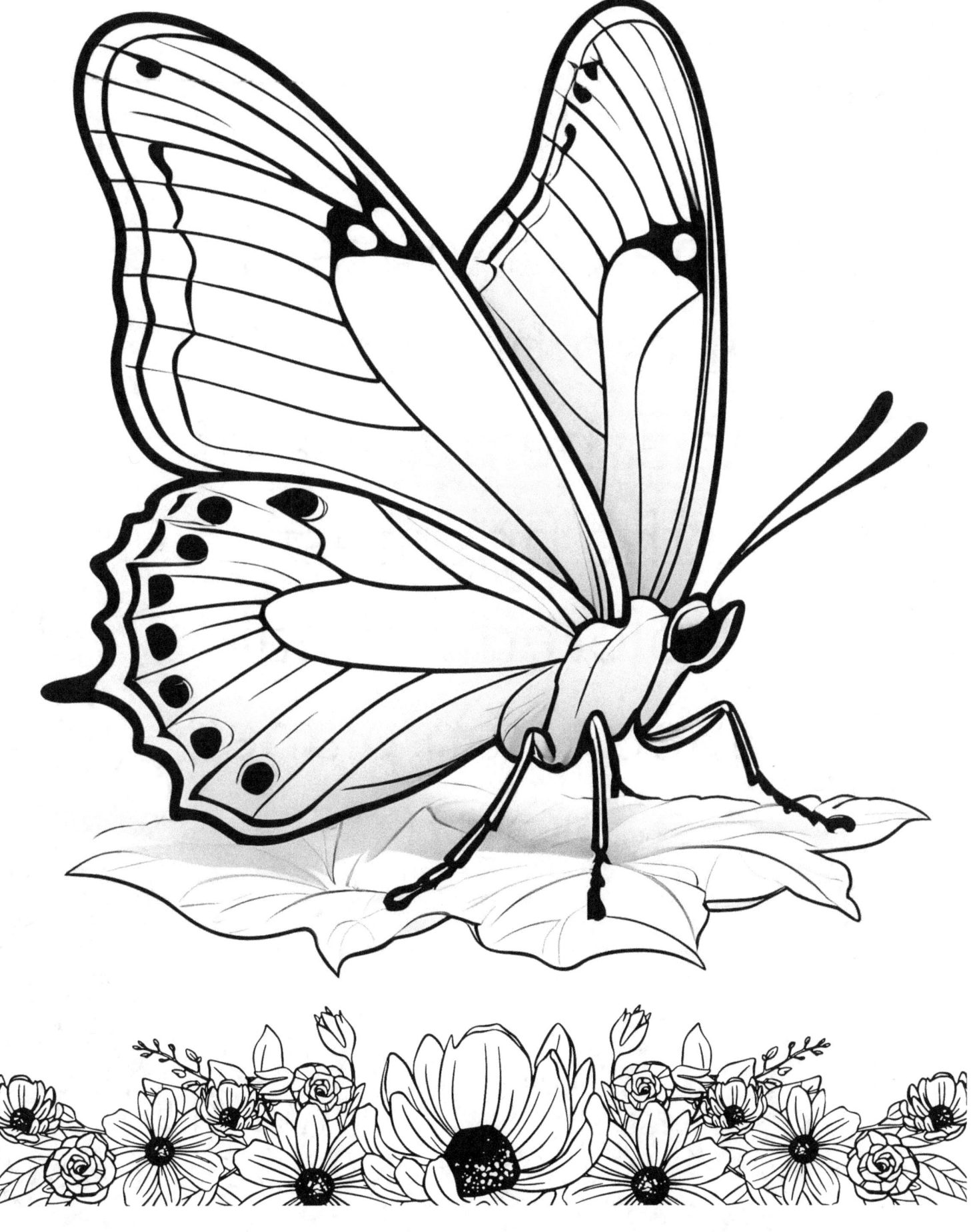

Emerald Butterfly. It can be seen in Asia, being one of the brightest colored animal species on planet Earth.

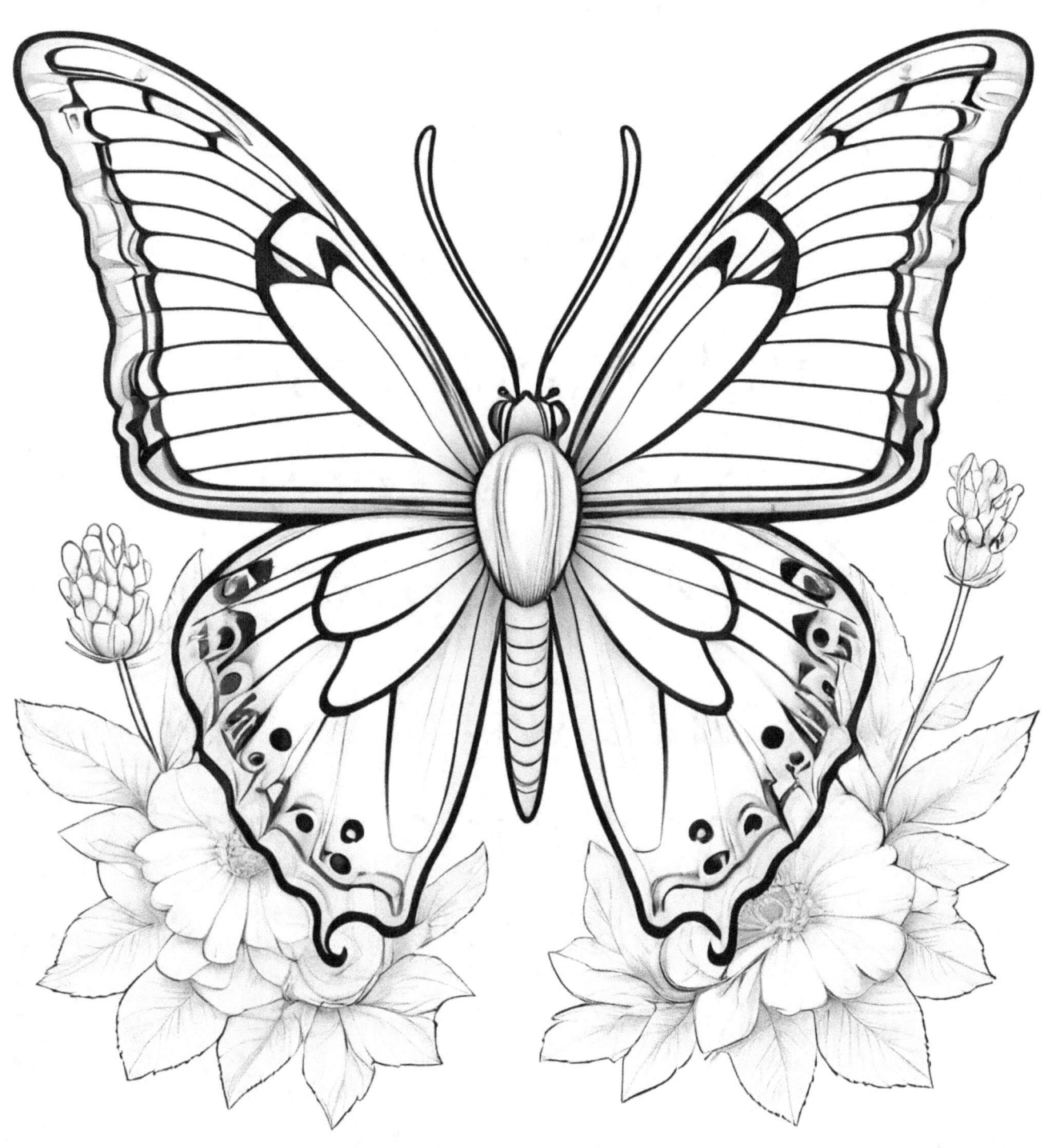

Butterflies undergo a complete metamorphosis, meaning they completely change their body form during their life cycle.

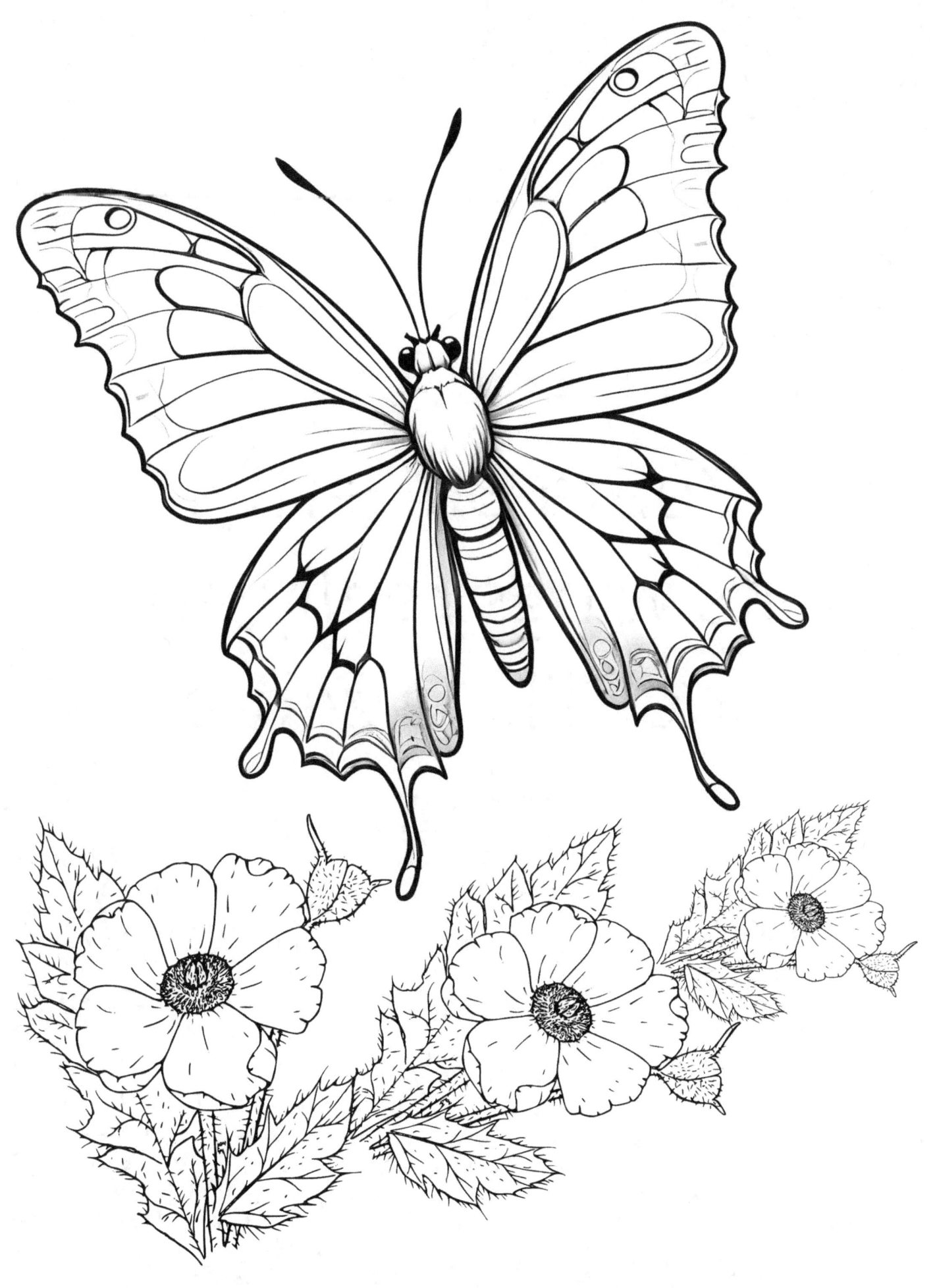

Zebra Butterfly. Its wings really do look like a zebra print.

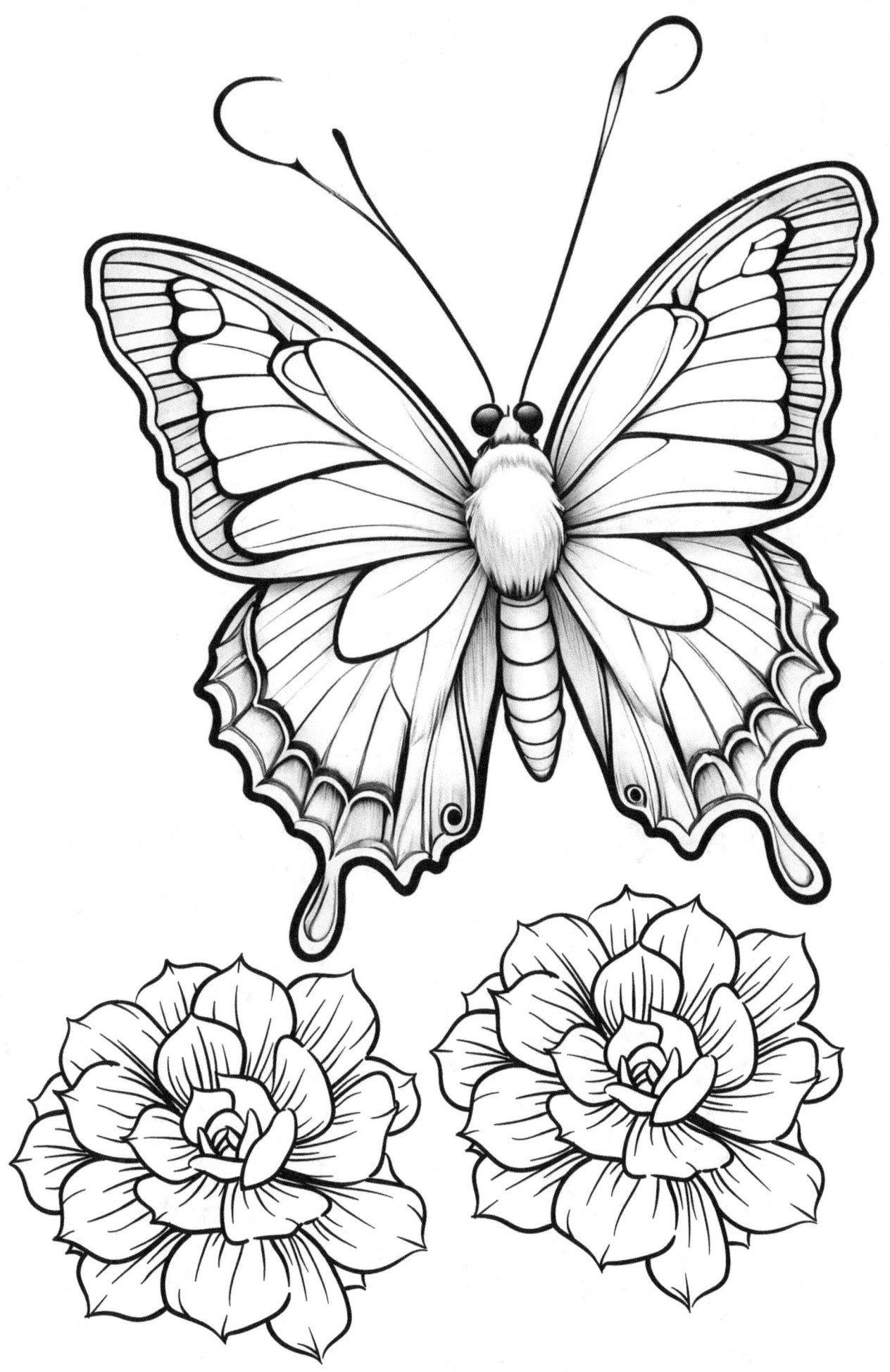

Butterflies cannot fly if their body temperature is below 86 degrees.

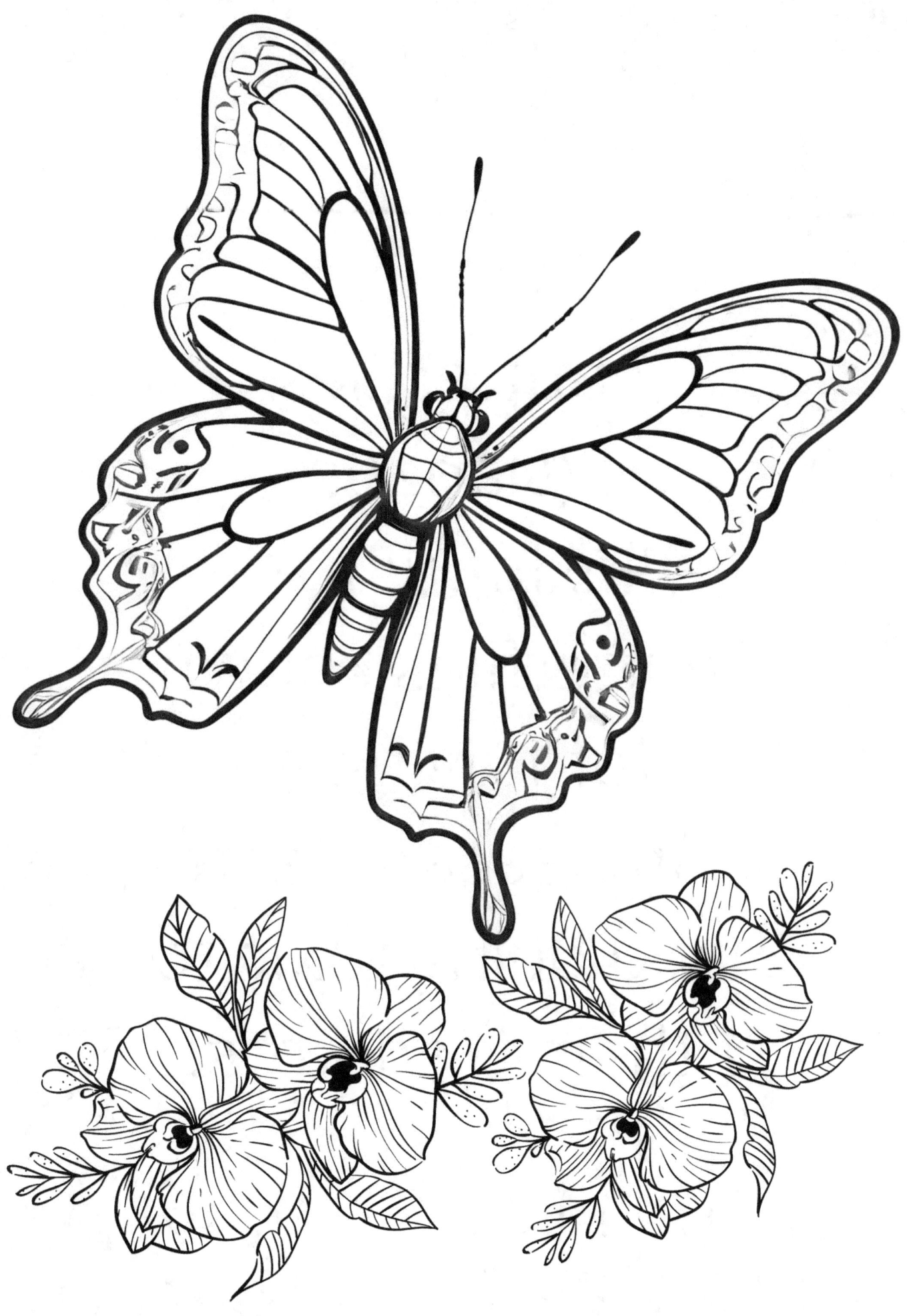

Monarch butterflies (Danaus Plexippus), are butterflies known for having an unpleasant taste and being toxic to their predators.

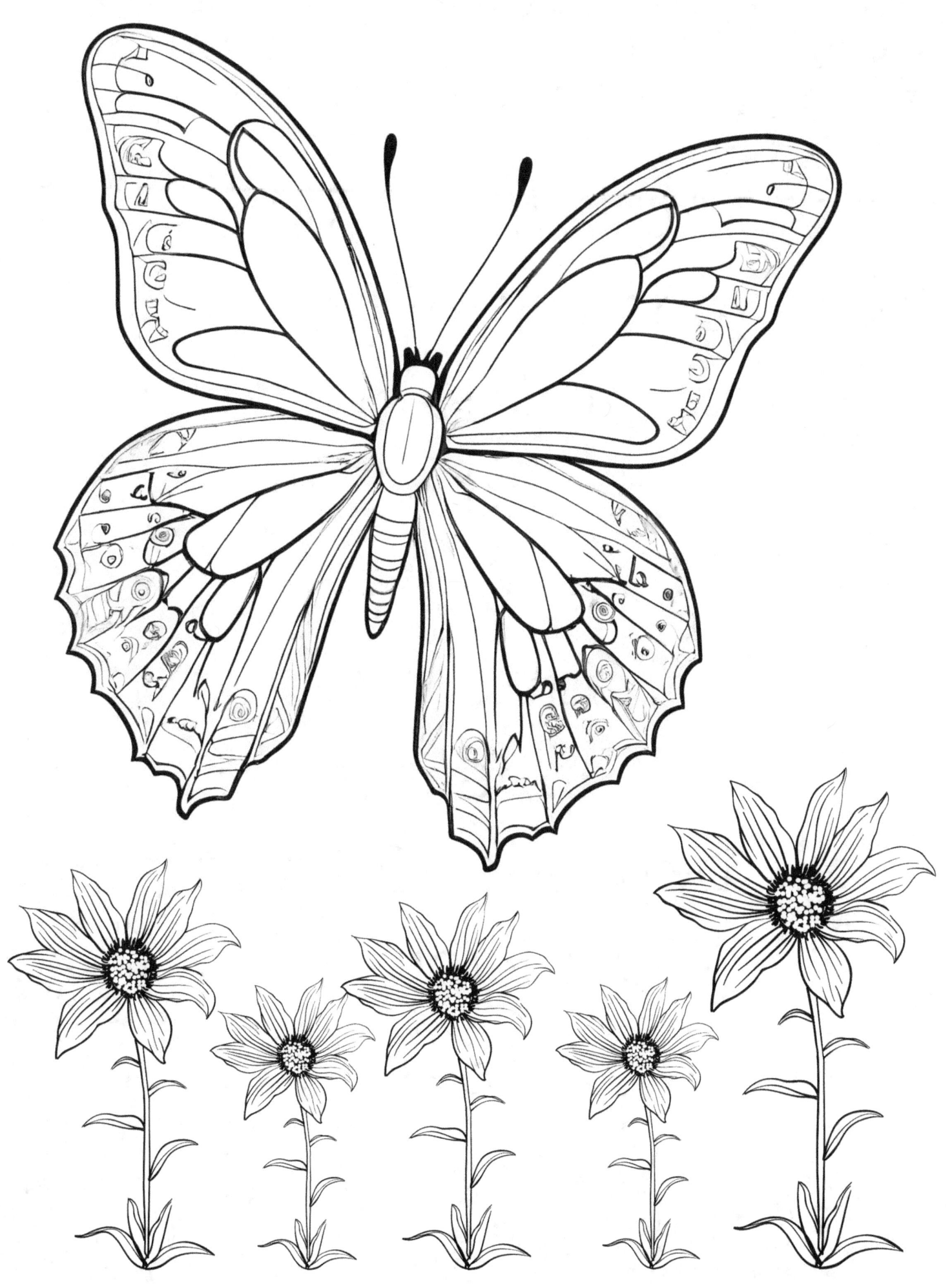

According to the analysis of genes and fossils, carried out by experts, butterflies appeared between 120 and 100 million years ago.

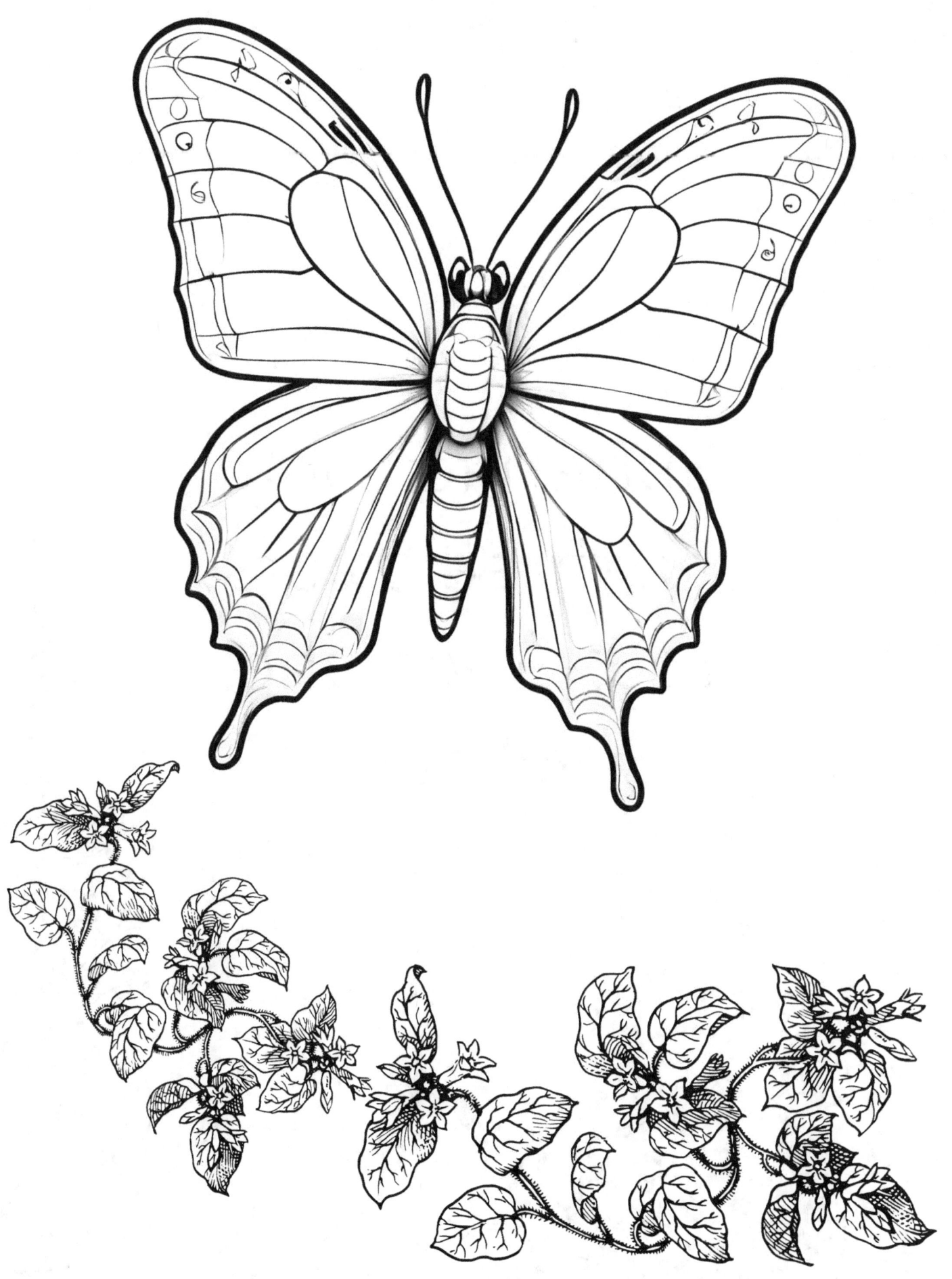

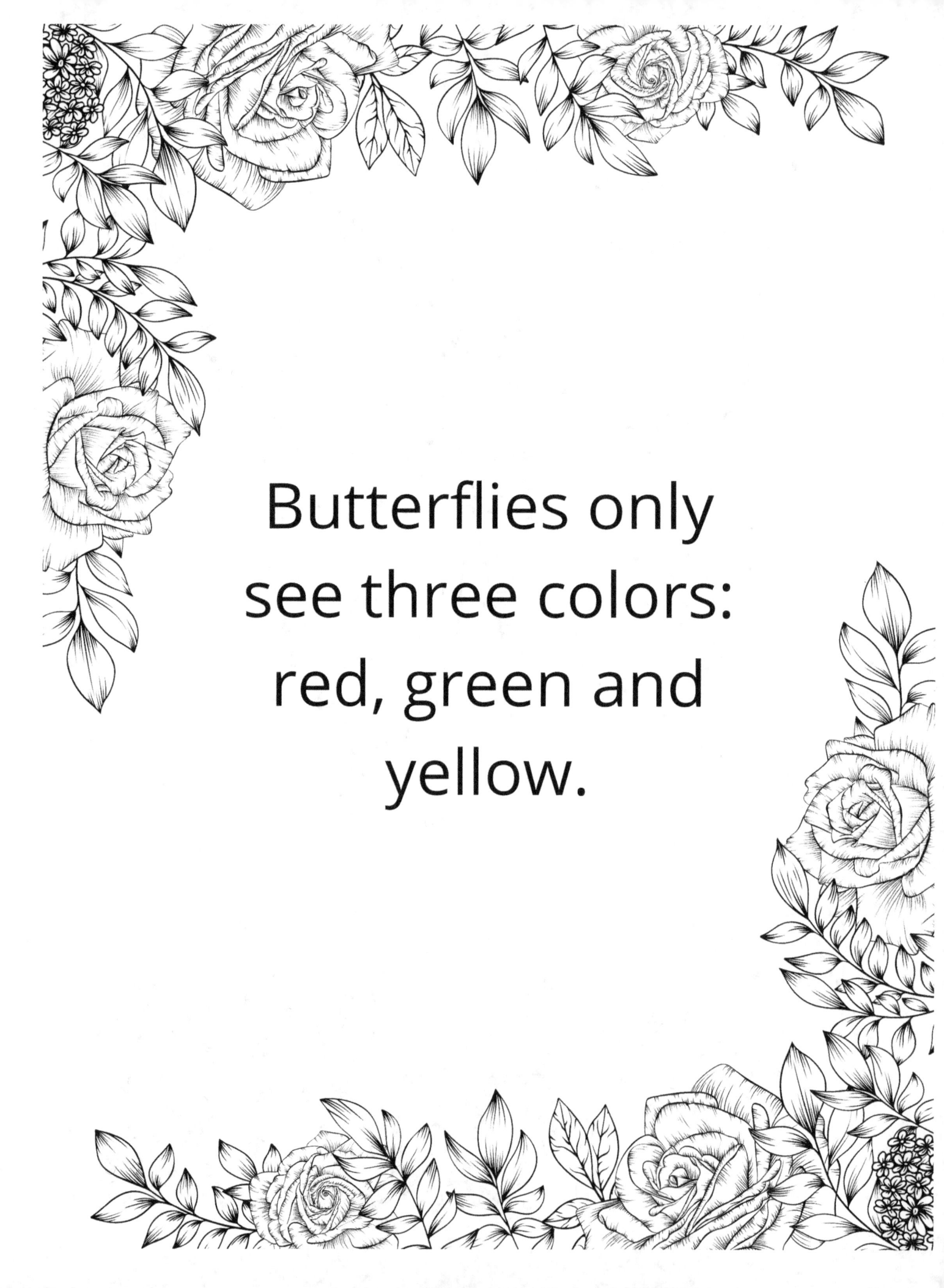

Butterflies only see three colors: red, green and yellow.

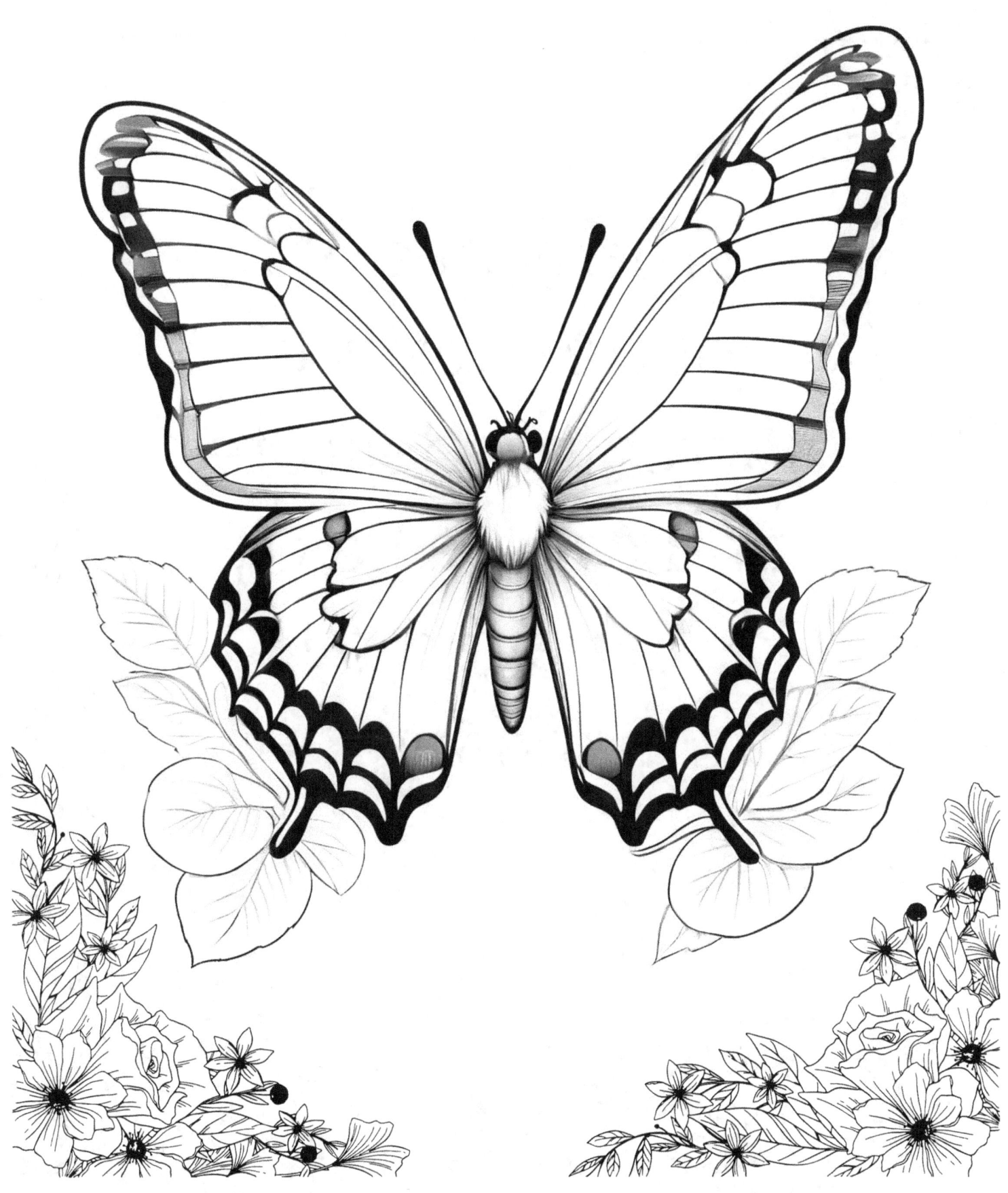

The wings of butterflies are incredibly delicate and can be easily damaged by handling.

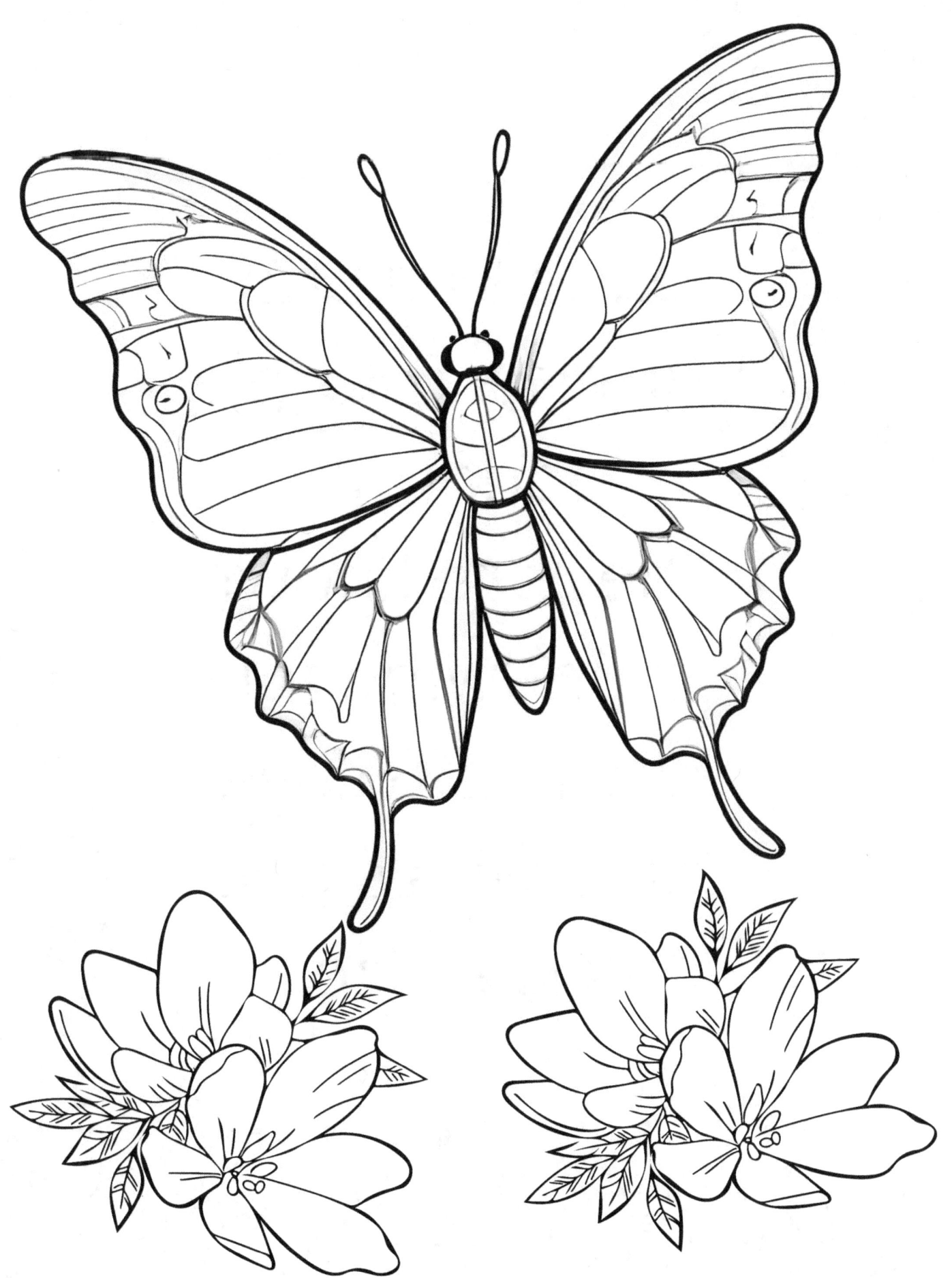

Blue Morpho Butterfly (Morpho godartii).
They are known worldwide for their reflective blue wings and large size.

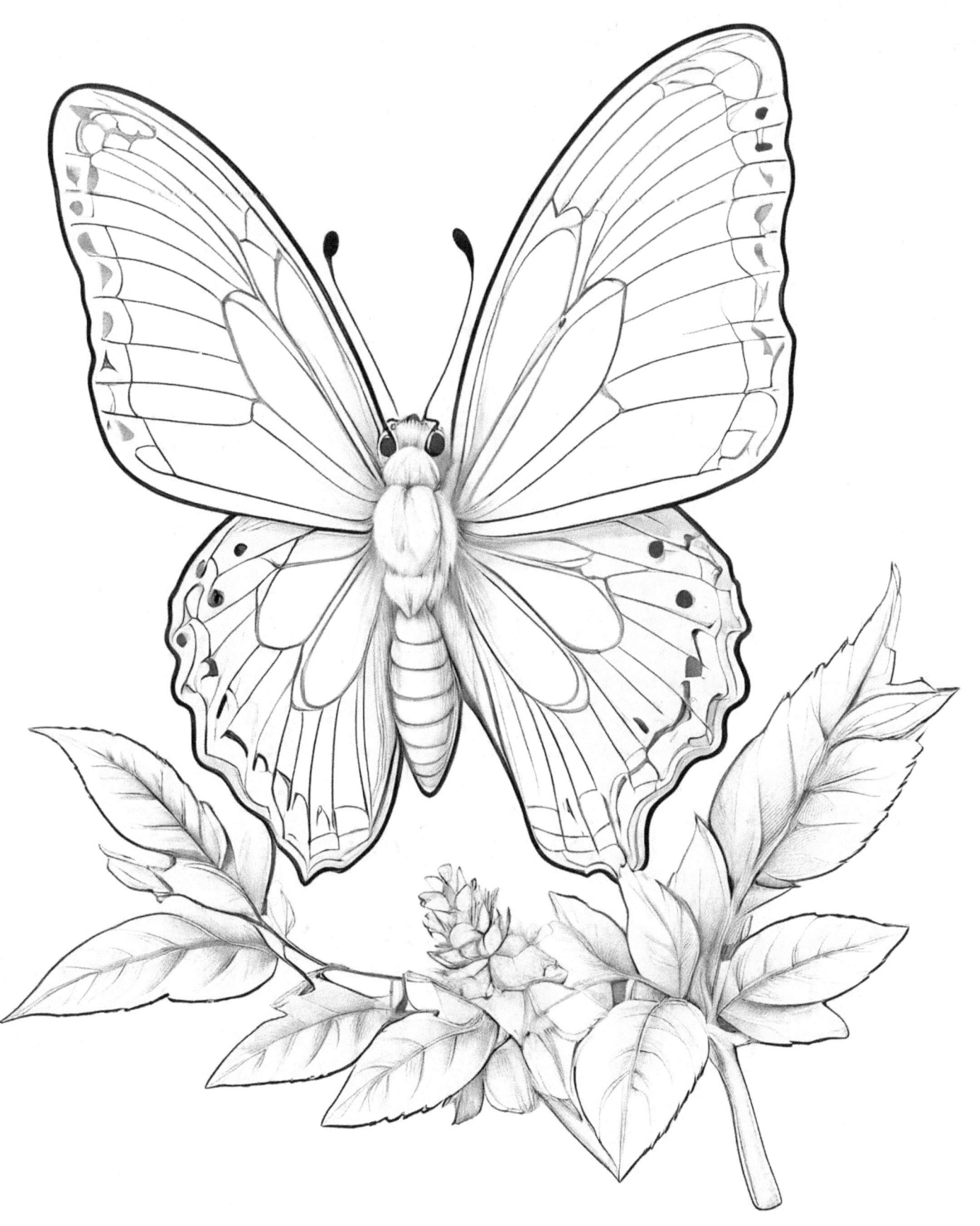

Buckeyana Butterfly (Prepona praeneste). This butterfly is so rare that it is almost impossible to find images of it on the Internet.

www.ingramcontent.com/pod-product-compliance
Lightning Source LLC
Chambersburg PA
CBHW082209220526
45470CB00010B/3104